# Finding God

## Our Response to God's Gifts

*As I open this book, I open myself*
*to God's presence in my life.*
*When I allow God's grace to help me,*
*I see with truth, hear with forgiveness,*
*and act with kindness.*
*Thank you God, for your presence in my life.*

Barbara F. Campbell, M.Div., D.Min.

James P. Campbell, M.A., D.Min.

**LOYOLA PRESS.**
A JESUIT MINISTRY
Chicago

| Imprimatur | In Conformity |
| --- | --- |
| In accordance with c. 827, permission to publish is granted on March 10, 2011 by Rev. Msgr. John F. Canary, Vicar General of the Archdiocese of Chicago. Permission to publish is an official declaration of ecclesiastical authority that the material is free from doctrinal and moral error. No legal responsibility is assumed by the grant of this permission. | The Subcommittee on the Catechism, United States Conference of Catholic Bishops, has found this catechetical text, copyright 2013, to be in conformity with the *Catechism of the Catholic Church*. |

*Finding God: Our Response to God's Gifts* is an expression of the work of Loyola Press, a ministry of the Chicago-Detroit Province of the Society of Jesus.

**Senior Consultants**
Jane Regan, Ph.D.
Richard Hauser, S.J., Ph.D., S.T.L.
Robert Fabing, S.J., D.Min.

**Advisors**
Most Reverend Gordon D. Bennett, S.J., D.D.
George A. Aschenbrenner, S.J., S.T.L.
Paul H. Colloton, O.P., D.Min.
Eugene LaVerdiere, S.S.S., Ph.D., S.T.L.
Gerald Darring, M.A.
Thomas J. McGrath, M.A.

**Catechetical Staff**
Jeanette L. Graham, M.A.
Jean Hopman, O.S.U., M.A.
Joseph Paprocki, D.Min.

Grateful acknowledgment is given to authors, publishers, photographers, museums, and agents for permission to reprint the following copyrighted material; music credits where appropriate can be found at the bottom of each individual song. Every effort has been made to determine copyright owners. In the case of any omissions, the publisher will be pleased to make suitable acknowledgments in future editions. Acknowledgments continue on page 259.

Cover design: Loyola Press
Cover Illustration: Rafael López
Interior design: Loyola Press and Think Bookworks

ISBN-13: 978-0-8294-3169-8
ISBN-10: 0-8294-3169-1

Manufactured in the United States of America.

LOYOLA PRESS.
A JESUIT MINISTRY

3441 N. Ashland Avenue
Chicago, Illinois 60657
(800) 621-1008

www.loyolapress.com
www.ignatianspirituality.com
www.other6.com

14 15 16 17 Web 10 9 8 7 6 5 4 3

# Contents

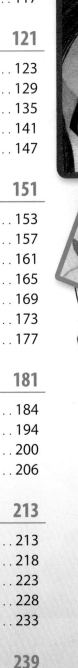

# God, Our Creator and Father

**Saint Francis of Assisi**

Saint Francis loved all living things.

# Saint Francis of Assisi

Francis liked the country. He loved the trees.
He loved the animals.

Once a hungry wolf began to bother people.
The people were scared.

Francis was not scared. He talked to "brother
wolf." He gave the wolf some food. Soon, no one
was scared. "Brother wolf" was everyone's friend.

Think about the wonderful world around you. Think about the animals. Think about the trees and flowers. Think about your friends and your family. What are your favorite things?

# God Makes Everything

## Prayer

*God, help me see the beauty of your world.*
*Help me always know that you love me.*

# God Is the Creator

**God** is the **Creator** of everything. God makes the sky and the sea. God makes trees and flowers. He even makes us.

God loves us. He wants us to enjoy everything he makes.

# Take Care of Our World

God loves us and wants us to be happy. How? We can love God and others. We can work together. We can play with one another. We can take care of our world.

We can show love for God by praying. When we have finished, we pray *Amen*.

Some people show love for God in a special way. Francis of Assisi did this. He was a **saint.**

Saint Francis of Assisi

GO TO PAGE 213

## Sign of the Cross

When we pray, we talk to God. We think of him. We ask God for what we need. We begin and end our prayer with the Sign of the Cross.

Show God your love. Talk with God in your heart. Tell him what you are thankful for.

*In the name of the Father,*

*and of the Son,*

*and of the Holy*

*Spirit.*

*Amen.*

# God Makes Good Things

God looked at everything he made. He saw green plants, sweet fruit, and fresh water. He said, "It is very good."

*adapted from Genesis 1:31*

Think about tall mountains, deep oceans, and animals of all sizes. Draw your favorite things God makes.

### Reading God's Word

Clouds play in the sky. Flowers bloom on earth. Trees bow their branches to God. All are happy. God is good. *adapted from Psalm 96:11–13*

# Faith Summary

God is the Creator of all people and all things. When we care for the world, we show God our love.

## Words I Learned

**Amen**       **God**
**Creator**    **saint**

## Ways of Being Like Jesus

Jesus shows that he loves God's world. *Show you love God's world. Pick up litter.*

### Prayer

*Thank you, God, for making this great world for us.*

## With My Family

*Activity* Plant flower or vegetable seeds in small paper cups. As a family, talk about how God creates everything. Discuss ways in which you as a family can care for God's world.

*Faith on the Go* Ask one another: *What is your favorite part of God's creation? Why?*

*Family Prayer* Dear God, bless our family and all of your creation. Help us care for your world. Amen.

Were you ever new to a group? Were you shy? Did someone help you feel welcome? How?

# God Cares for Us

## Prayer

*Loving God, teach me to care for others. Help me show your love to them.*

# Showing God We Care

Together at **Mass** we hear stories about God. We pray together. We sing together. We show our love for God.

At Mass we pray together to celebrate the wonderful things God does for us. Mass is a special kind of **liturgy**.

### Reading God's Word

I will enjoy the good things God has given me.

*adapted from Psalm 27:13*

God gives us so many wonderful things. At Mass we praise God for who he is and thank God for all he does. We use our voices to sing and our hearts to express our love. Together as one family at Mass, we celebrate God's love through prayer.

Draw your favorite part of the Mass.

GO TO
PAGE
214

## We Give Thanks

We give thanks to God with special words. These are words you can pray.

### We Praise You

*We praise you.*
*We bless you.*
*We thank you.*

God loves and cares for you. You are so special!

In your heart, talk with God. Thank him for the way he cares for you.

# God's Perfect World

God said, "I give you all the plants and trees.

They have seeds and fruit for you to eat."

*adapted from Genesis 1:29*

How do we know God cares for us? He gives us good things.

## God Gives Us Good Things

Name the good things in the picture. Then color the picture.

## Faith Summary

God loves us. He loves us more than anyone else can.
God wants us to love one another.

| Words I Learned | Ways of Being Like Jesus |
|---|---|
| liturgy<br>Mass | Jesus cares for others. *Show others you care about them.* |

### Prayer

*Thank you, God, for loving me and caring for me.*

## With My Family

*Activity* Draw a picture of a time you and
your family showed love to someone.

*Faith on the Go* Ask one another: *Where is
your favorite place to pray? Why?*

*Family Prayer* *Dear God, bless our family. Help
us know how much you love us so that we can
share your love with others. Amen.*

Whose birthday is it? How is the family showing love? Think of your family. How can you show your love?

# God Is Our Father

**Prayer**

*God, help me learn about your love. Help me grow closer to you.*

# A Special Message

Today is Ben's birthday. His father gives him a special card.

Did you ever get a special message?
How did you feel?

Happy Birthday

Dear Ben,
You are very special to me.
You are kind to our family.
I will love you always.
                    Dad

# God's Message

God our Father sends us a message. He loves and cares for us. God's message is in the **Bible.** The Bible is the story of God's promise to care for us. It also tells us about **Jesus,** God's Son.

Connect the dots below and discover the hidden image. Write the name of the picture you have drawn.

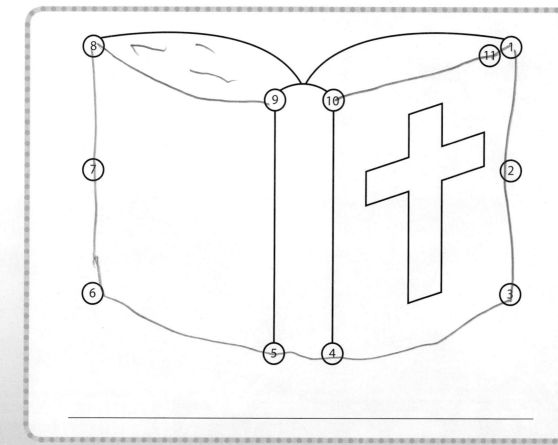

_____

## Link to Liturgy

At Mass we hear stories from the Bible.

GO TO PAGE 215

## How Special You Are

Imagine Jesus is speaking to you, telling you how special you are! He tells you how much God loves you. Jesus tells you this is God's message in the Bible.

Meet Jesus in your heart. Talk with him. Know that he hears your words. Be still with Jesus.

# A Home with Jesus

Imagine Jesus is coming to your home. How do you greet him? Who else is there to welcome him? What do you do when he comes?

Draw a picture of Jesus in your home.

## Reading God's Word

Jesus said, "If you love me, my Father will love you. We will live with you in love."

*adapted from John 14:23*

# Faith Summary

God our Father and his Son, Jesus, speak to us in a special way. We learn about God's love in the Bible.

**Words I Learned**

**Bible**

**Jesus**

**Ways of Being Like Jesus**

Jesus tells us that God loves us. *Share God's message. Say "God loves you." Say "I love you too."*

## Prayer

*Thank you, God, for your message in the Bible.*

## With My Family

**Activity** Put your family Bible in a special place. Ask your mom or dad to read with you.

**Faith on the Go** Ask one another: *What are some ways to show your love for God?*

**Family Prayer** *Dear God, bless our family. Thank you for sharing your words in the Bible. Amen.*

Think about your friends. How do you feel when you play together?

# God Gives Us Peace

### *Prayer*

*God, help me live in peace. I want to share your peace with others.*

21

# A Gift of Peace

Jesus' friends were in a room. Jesus came to see them. He said, "Peace be with you. My Father sent me to you. Now I send you to help others." He breathed on them. Then he said, "The **Holy Spirit** is with you." *adapted from John 20:19–22*

Jesus gives us the Holy Spirit. The Holy Spirit is always with us. He brings us God's peace.

## All Are One

The Father, the Son, and the
Holy Spirit are the **Trinity.**

*God our Father made us.*

*Jesus, his Son, brings us God's love.*

*The Holy Spirit brings us peace.*

God made us out of love.
Love and peace are God's gifts to us.

GO TO
PAGE
216

## Give Praise

We praise the Trinity when we pray.

### Glory Be to the Father

*Glory be to the Father,*
*and to the Son,*
*and to the Holy Spirit.*
*As it was in the beginning,*
*is now, and ever shall be,*
*world without end.*
*Amen.*

God is always with us. Talk with God in your heart. Tell him how you will share his peace with others.

# Father, Son, and Holy Spirit

What do we call the Father, the Son, and the Holy Spirit? Color the spaces that have dots. Then read the words.

### ❓ Did You Know?

When you see a friend, what do you say? When Saint Francis saw a friend, he said something special. He said, "Peace and goodness." Try it!

# Faith Summary

God is always with us. God our Father made us. Jesus, his Son, brings us God's love. The Holy Spirit brings us peace.

| Words I Learned | Ways of Being Like Jesus |
|---|---|
| **Holy Spirit** | Jesus brings us God's love. |
| **Trinity** | *You can bring God's love. You can share your toys.* |

## Prayer

*Thank you, Holy Spirit, for bringing peace to my life.*

## With My Family

*Activity* Talk with your family at dinner. Pray a quiet prayer of thanks for your wonderful family and the time you share together.

*Faith on the Go* Ask one another: *How can you show God's love?*

*Family Prayer* *Dear God, bless my family and help us always know how much you love us.*

# Celebrating Ordinary Time

The Church keeps a calendar to mark different seasons and special times in Jesus' life. We call the Church's year the **liturgical year.**

We celebrate **Ordinary Time** two times during each liturgical year. We celebrate first between the Christmas season and Lent, then again from summer until fall.

**Prayer**

*Dear Jesus, I know you are my friend. Help me to grow closer to you.*

## We Show Thanks During Ordinary Time

Ordinary Time is a time to be grateful for all living things. All living things grow. We grow by learning more about Jesus. We grow by showing our love for Jesus and for others. We also give thanks and praise to God for all the gifts he gives us.

Draw a picture of one gift God has given you.

Thank you, God!

### Reading God's Word

Give thanks to God.  *adapted from 1 Corinthians 1:4*

# Mass During Ordinary Time

When we go to Mass during Ordinary Time, we celebrate God's **creation.** We give thanks for all that God makes for us. We show our thanks by caring for God's creation.

## What We Experience

We see flowers or plants around the altar. We also see the gifts of Bread and Wine. The gifts of Bread and Wine are offered at every Mass.

### God's Special Gifts

Circle the two gifts that are offered at every Mass.

**Did You Know?**

The liturgical color for Ordinary Time is green.

GO TO PAGE 217

## Living My Faith

# Faith Summary

Ordinary Time is a time to be grateful for all of God's gifts.

### Words I Learned

**creation**
**liturgical year**
**Ordinary Time**

### Ways of Being Like Jesus

Jesus loves God's creation. *Take care of people, plants, and animals.*

## Prayer

*Dear Jesus, thank you for helping me to love all of God's gifts.*

## With My Family

**Activity** When you go to Mass during Ordinary Time, look around your church. Find examples of things described on page 29.

**Faith on the Go** Ask one another: *What gifts did God bless me with?*

**Family Prayer** Invite your family to use Ordinary Time to grow in faith together. Make a prayer jar for special prayers or requests.

# Jesus, Our Lord and Savior

## Saint Joseph

Saint Joseph was Jesus' foster father.

He was a good man, and he loved God.

# Saint Joseph

Joseph was a carpenter.
He worked hard.

Mary was Joseph's wife.
She was going to have a baby.

An angel spoke to Joseph.
The angel said Mary's baby
would be called Jesus.

Joseph cared for Jesus and
Mary for the rest of his life.

David has a baby sister. Her name is Mary Kate.

Do you have a baby sister or baby brother? Do you remember when he or she was born? How did you feel?

# God Sends Jesus

## Prayer

*Loving God, show me how to always welcome Jesus into my heart.*

# Jesus Is Born

**Mary** was going to have a baby. She and **Joseph** were far from home. They had no place to sleep for the night. Imagine how they felt.

Mary and Joseph stayed in a stable. This is where Jesus, the Son of God, was born.

It was a special time when Jesus was born. Shepherds were in the fields. God sent his messengers, the **angels,** to the shepherds. The angels sang songs. They told the shepherds where to find Jesus.

*adapted from Luke 2:4–14*

### ? Did You Know?

The name *Jesus* means "God saves." God sent Jesus to save us.

# The Holy Family

God sent us his only Son, Jesus. Joseph and Mary cared for him. We call Jesus, Mary, and Joseph the **Holy Family.**

Mary and Joseph loved Jesus very much. They taught him many things about God. They took care of Jesus every day. Jesus obeyed Mary and Joseph. They were a happy family who loved one another and learned many things from one another.

Think about your family and the things you've learned from them.

## My Family Loves Me

Draw something you've learned from someone in your family.

GO TO PAGE 218

## Prayer to the Holy Family

Imagine you are with the Holy Family. You are in the stable where Jesus was born.

Look around. What is it like? Ask Mary and Joseph if you may hold their new baby.

Jesus is in your arms. You hold him against your heart. What do you want to say to him? Let Jesus know how much you love him. Then give him back to Mary and Joseph.

## Who's Who

Think about the Holy Family. Mary was a kind and loving mother. Joseph was a gentle and warm foster father. Jesus, the Son of God, grew up as their child.

Look at the pictures below. Write the name of each person on the line.

_____

# The Holy Family

_____

## Faith Summary

God wanted to show us his love. He sent us his Son, Jesus. Joseph and Mary were Jesus' parents on earth. Jesus needed them both.

**Words I Learned**

angel
**Holy Family**
**Joseph**
Mary

**Ways of Being Like Jesus**

Jesus loved Mary and Joseph.
*Tell your parents you love them.*

# I love you.

### Prayer

*Thank you, God, for sending us Jesus.*

## With My Family

**Activity** Ask your family about the day you were born. What was it like?

**Faith on the Go** Ask one another: *If you could ask Mary one question, what would it be?*

**Family Prayer** *Dear God, bless our family like you blessed the Holy Family. Help us to live by their example.*

On the way home, Emma fell asleep in the car. Dad carried her into the house and to her room.

When did someone take care of you? What did he or she do for you? How did you feel?

# Jesus Teaches Us

## Prayer

*Caring Jesus, guide me when I talk to God. I want to be close to him.*

# Jesus Prayed to God

Jesus both talked to and listened to God. When we pray a **prayer,** we talk to God and listen to him in our hearts. Jesus gave us a special prayer called the Lord's Prayer. When we pray it, we grow closer to God, Jesus, and one another.

### Reading God's Word

Jesus went up the mountain to pray. All night long he prayed to God.

*adapted from Luke 6:12*

# The Lord's Prayer

The Lord's Prayer is very important. Listen for it at Mass. It starts like this.

Our Father, — — — → God is our Father.

who art in **heaven,** — — → Heaven is life with God.

hallowed be thy name; — → God's name is holy.

thy kingdom come, — — → We live as Jesus teaches us.

thy will be done — — → We ask God to guide us.

on earth as it is in heaven. — — → We pray that people will do what is pleasing to God.

GO TO PAGE 219

## Lord's Prayer

*Our Father, who art in heaven,*
*hallowed be thy name;*
*thy kingdom come,*
*thy will be done*
*on earth as it is in heaven.*

Talk to Jesus in your heart. Thank him for teaching you how to pray. Tell Jesus you will talk with God and listen as he did.

# Serving God's Kingdom

We are called to serve the Kingdom of God. You serve the Kingdom of God when you do good things for others.

Put an X next to the picture if someone is serving the Kingdom of God.

# Faith Summary

Jesus taught us the Lord's Prayer. It is our most important prayer.

| Words I Learned | Ways of Being Like Jesus |
| --- | --- |
| **Heaven** | Jesus taught his friends how to pray. |
| **Kingdom of God*** | *Ask Jesus to help you pray.* |
| **prayer** | |

### Prayer

*Thank you, Jesus, for teaching me how to pray. I will talk to God every day.*

## With My Family

**Activity** Pray with your family at bedtime.

**Faith on the Go** Ask one another: *Where is your favorite place to pray the Lord's Prayer?*

**Family Prayer** *Dear God, thank you for sharing your special prayer with us. Be with us as we try to live by your words.*

If you had one wish, what would you wish for? Is it something you really need? What about a big hug when you are sad? What about laughter with a friend?

# Trust in God

**Prayer**

*Jesus, my friend, help me trust God in all things.*

# Learning the Lord's Prayer

We learned how the Lord's Prayer begins.

*Our Father, who art in heaven,*
*hallowed be thy name;*
*thy kingdom come,*
*thy will be done*
*on earth as it is in heaven.*

Now we will learn the rest.

| | |
|---|---|
| *Give us this day our daily bread,* → | We ask God to give us what we need. |
| *and forgive us our* **trespasses,** → | We ask God to forgive us for hurting others. |
| *as we forgive those who trespass against us;* → | We ask God to help us forgive those who have hurt us. |
| *and lead us not into* **temptation,** → | We ask God to help us make good decisions. |
| *but deliver us from evil.* → | We ask God to protect us. |
| *Amen.* → | We say yes to God. |

*adapted from Matthew 6:9–13*

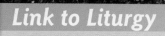

### Link to Liturgy

We always pray the Lord's Prayer at Mass. Sometimes we sing it. Sometimes we speak it.

GO TO PAGE 220

## Pray the Lord's Prayer

The Lord's Prayer helps us tell God what we need.

*Our Father, who art in heaven,*
*hallowed be thy name;*
*thy kingdom come,*
*thy will be done*
*on earth as it is in heaven.*
*Give us this day our daily bread,*
*and forgive us our trespasses,*
*as we forgive those who trespass against us;*
*and lead us not into temptation,*
*but deliver us from evil.*
*Amen.*

Think about what you just asked God to do for you. Thank him for giving you what you need.

# Needs or Wants?

God wants us to have everything we need. What do you really need?

Circle the things you really need.

## Reading God's Word

God is happy to give you his kingdom.

*adapted from Luke 12:32*

# Faith Summary

In the Lord's Prayer, we ask God to give us what we need. We ask him to protect us. We ask him to forgive us and to help us forgive others.

## Words I Learned

temptation

trespasses

## Ways of Being Like Jesus

Jesus asked God only for what he truly needed. *Ask God only for what you truly need.*

### Prayer

*Thank you, God, for giving me what I need.*

## With My Family

**Activity** Give your family something they need. Give Mom or Dad a big hug just because.

**Faith on the Go** Ask one another: *What is one thing you need from God every day?*

**Family Prayer** *Dear God, please bless my family. Thank you for the wonderful things you give us every day.*

Amy could not find her puppy. She looked upstairs. She looked downstairs. Amy looked all morning. Tears rolled down her face.

Then Amy heard a bark at the door. Amy was so happy! Did you ever find something you had lost? How did you feel?

# Jesus Rises from the Dead

### Prayer

*Dear Jesus, help me remember you are always with me.*

# Jesus Is Risen

When Jesus died, his friends were sad. They missed him very much. Two women went to his tomb. An angel was there. The women were scared.

The angel said, "Do not be afraid. I know you are looking for Jesus. You think he is dead, but he is not. Jesus **Christ** is alive! Go tell your friends."

The women were full of joy! They ran to tell their friends.

On the way, the women saw Jesus Christ. He was walking on the road. The women were so happy! They cried with joy.

Jesus said, "Do not be afraid. Tell my friends to go into town. I will see them there."

*adapted from Matthew 28:1–10*

 **Reading God's Word**

Whenever people come together for me, I am with them.

*adapted from Matthew 18:20*

GO TO PAGE 221

## Be with Jesus

Jesus is always with you. He is with you when you think about him. He is with you when you pray.

Meet Jesus in your favorite place. Take time to talk with him. What would you like to say? What does Jesus want you to know?

Take a few moments to enjoy having Jesus so close. Tell him how happy you are that he is with you.

## Finding Jesus

Help the women find the tomb. Then help them
find Jesus Christ.

# Faith Summary

When Jesus died, his friends were sad. Then they found out Jesus was alive. They were so happy! They prayed and talked together.

**Words I Learned**

**Christ**
**Resurrection***

**Ways of Being Like Jesus**

Jesus is always here with us. *Take time to talk to Jesus and listen to him in your heart.*

## Prayer

*Jesus, my friend, thank you for always being close to me.*

## With My Family

**Activity** Surprise your parents. Write them a note. Put it on a mirror where they will see it.

**Faith on the Go** Ask one another: *Where is a special place you like to go to talk with Jesus?*

**Family Prayer** Dear God, thank you for our wonderful family. Help us always be good friends to everyone we meet.

# Celebrating Advent

Each liturgical year we **celebrate Advent.**
Advent is the season before Christmas.
Advent is four weeks long.

**Prayer**

*Dear Jesus, help me to show love each week of Advent.*

# We Prepare During Advent

Advent is a time to get ready to celebrate Jesus' birth. Each day of Advent we get ready to welcome Jesus.

During Advent, how will you prepare your heart for Jesus? Draw a picture inside each heart.

I Pray.

I Share.

I Love.

 **Reading God's Word**

God loves us so much that he sent us Jesus.

*adapted from John 3:16*

# Mass During Advent

When you go to Mass during Advent, your church may have a large Advent wreath. The wreath has four candles. Usually three of the candles are purple and one is pink.

## What We Experience

Each week one more candle is lit, making the Advent wreath brighter. We're waiting for Jesus, the **Light of the World.** A lit candle helps us see in the dark. Jesus, the Light of the World, helps us see how much God loves us.

Color the Advent wreath and the candles.

### Link to Liturgy

We do not sing the *Gloria* on Sundays during Advent.

GO TO PAGE 222

## Living My Faith

# Faith Summary

Advent is a time to get ready to celebrate Jesus' birth.

Each day of Advent we get ready to welcome Jesus into our hearts.

| Words I Learned | Ways of Being Like Jesus |
| --- | --- |
| **Advent** | Jesus loves and welcomes everyone. |
| **celebrate** | *Invite a new friend over to play.* |
| **Light of the World** | |

## Prayer

*Dear Jesus, we are so happy and thankful that you were born!*

## With My Family

*Activity* When you go to Mass during Advent, look around your church. Look for the Advent wreath. Talk about what you see.

*Faith on the Go* Ask one another: *What will you do this Advent to prepare for Christmas?*

*Family Prayer* Use Advent to invite family members to grow in faith. Set up an Advent wreath at home. Take time each week to light the candles and pray together as a family.

# The Church, Our Community in the Spirit

## Saint Peter

Saint Peter was one of Jesus' best friends.

# Saint Peter

Long ago there was a fisherman. His name was Peter. Jesus said to him, "Come, follow me." So Peter left his work. He followed Jesus.

Peter loved Jesus. Peter tried to be like Jesus. Sometimes Peter didn't do the right thing. But Jesus always forgave him.

Jesus asked Peter to care for his friends. Peter said yes. So Jesus made Peter the leader of all his people.

**Saint Peter, Aix Cathedral, France**

Think about a friend of yours. Think about the first time he or she asked you to play. How did you feel?

# Following Jesus

### Prayer

*Jesus, my friend, show me how to follow you. I want to help others.*

# The Church

Today we find Jesus' friends in the **Church.** We follow Jesus together. We learn to love one another. We learn to love others in the world. When we come together, the Holy Spirit is with us. He fills us with God's life and love.

Haiti

Philippines

India

Mexico

The Church has angels watching over it. So do you! Your **guardian angel** is an angel who watches over you and guides your steps every day.

### My Guardian Angel

Draw a picture of your guardian angel. Every time you look at your picture, remember that your guardian angel helps you.

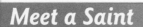

### Meet a Saint

Saint Michael is a great angel. He cares for police officers and for our Church. You have a special angel caring for you too.

GO TO PAGE 223

## Pray to Follow Jesus

Imagine you are playing. You hear someone call your name. You look up. It is Jesus. He asks, "Will you help me? Help me show God's love to others."

Jesus said this to the fishermen. Think about how they trusted Jesus to lead them.

Now spend some time with Jesus. He asks you to help him too. How will you answer Jesus?

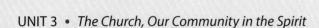

# People in Your Church

Jesus' friends are in the Church. Draw them.
Draw yourself too.

## Living My Faith

# Faith Summary

Jesus gave us the Church. We find Jesus' friends here. We learn to love others here.

**Words I Learned**

**Church**

**guardian angel**

**Ways of Being Like Jesus**

Jesus cares for us and helps us. *Teach your friends to show God's love to others. Set a good example and be nice to everyone.*

### Prayer

*Jesus, my friend, thank you for asking me to help you.*

## With My Family

*Activity* Smile when you meet Jesus' friends at church.

*Faith on the Go* Ask one another: *What words would you use to ask a friend to follow Jesus with you?*

*Family Prayer* *Dear Jesus, bless my friends and family who make up your Church. Be with us as we learn to help one another.*

What is a surprise?
Have you ever received
a wonderful surprise?
How did you feel?

# Jesus Sends the Holy Spirit

### Prayer

*Caring Jesus, help me know the Holy Spirit. I will let the Holy Spirit guide me.*

# The Holy Spirit Is with Us

God the Father, God the Son, and God the Holy Spirit are the three Persons of the Trinity. Just as God and Jesus love and care for us, so does the Holy Spirit.

The Holy Spirit is with us in our **parish.** A parish is our community of family and friends who come together to worship God.

The Holy Spirit comes to all of us when we are baptized. He never leaves us. He is with us at home, at school, at the park—everywhere!

The Holy Spirit is with us when we are kind and help others. He guides us to do the right thing.

### Did You Know?

The Holy Spirit is like the wind. We cannot see him, but he is with us. Try blowing on a piece of paper. What happens?

### Gifts of the Spirit

The Holy Spirit is with us always and brings us wonderful gifts. Color the words below that name some of these gifts.

## Kindness Love

## Holy Spirit

## Peace Caring

GO TO PAGE 224

## Pray to the Holy Spirit

Think of a kind thing you did. The Holy Spirit helped you to be kind. We can pray to the Holy Spirit.

*In the name of the Father,
and of the Son,
and of the Holy Spirit.
Amen.*

The Holy Spirit lives in your heart. Talk with him. Thank him for being your friend. Ask him to help you be more loving.

# The Story of the Holy Spirit

The Holy Spirit first came to Jesus' friends as a surprise. They did not expect his visit or the wonderful gift he brought them.

Fill in the blanks with the correct words. Look at the pictures for help.

> Jesus    praying    friends    wind    fire

1. One day Jesus' _____ were together.

2. They were _____.

3. A big _____ came from the sky.

4. They saw flames of _____, but they were not afraid.

5. Then they told the world about _____.

# Living My Faith

## Faith Summary

The Holy Spirit is always with us. He helps us be kind. He helps us be loving.

### Words I Learned

parish
Pentecost*

### Ways of Being Like Jesus

Jesus showed his unending kindness when he gave us the Holy Spirit. *Do kind deeds for others. Help someone with a chore or task without being asked.*

### Prayer

*Kind Jesus, I am grateful for the gift of the Holy Spirit in my life.*

### With My Family

**Activity** Talk about a happy surprise you received. What was it? How did you feel?

**Faith on the Go** Ask one another: *How can you thank the Holy Spirit for always being with you?*

**Family Prayer** *Dear God, we're so blessed to have you with us every day. Help us to always follow you.*

What does it mean to share? What do you share with others? What are you showing others when you share with them?

# Jesus Teaches Us to Share

### Prayer

*Loving Jesus, teach me how to share. I will share your love with others.*

# Sharing with Others

After the Holy Spirit came, Jesus' friends were happy. They were ready to share Jesus' love.

They ate together and prayed together. They shared their food and money. They shared everything they had. They even shared what they knew about Jesus. People loved this way of life. Every day more people joined them.    *adapted from Acts of the Apostles 2:42–47*

### Reading God's Word

Be happy, and share your happiness.

*adapted from Philippians 2:18*

## Who We Are

We call the first friends of Jesus Christ **Christians.** We are Christians too.

We belong to the **Catholic** Church. As Catholics we share and pray together. Jesus' friends did this long ago. Jesus' friends still do this today.

How do we share our love at Mass? One way is to offer the sign of peace to the people around us. Jesus shared his peace with his friends when he said: "Peace be with you."

What are the children on this page sharing? Trace the word to find the answer.

Peace

GO TO PAGE 225

## Prayer

### Pray to Jesus

This is a special prayer to Jesus.

*Thank you, Jesus.*
*My friend! My brother!*
*Help me know you more clearly.*
*Help me love you more dearly.*
*Help me follow you more nearly.*
*Amen.*

*adapted from Saint Richard of Chichester's Prayer*

Imagine you are with Jesus. He is smiling at you. Tell Jesus how you will love him. Tell him how you will follow him.

# What Can You Share?

Draw a picture in each box of things you can share.

I can share
with my friends.

I can share
with my family.

I can share
with my neighbors.

I can share
at Mass.

# Faith Summary

We belong to the Catholic Church. We show our love by sharing with others.

### Words I Learned

**Catholic**

**Christian**

### Ways of Being Like Jesus

Jesus shared what he had. *Share a favorite toy or treat with a brother, sister, or friend.*

### Prayer

*Jesus, my teacher, thank you for teaching me how to share.*

## With My Family

*Activity* Talk about a time you shared something even though it wasn't easy to do.

*Faith on the Go* Ask one another: *What is something you can share to show your love?*

*Family Prayer* *Dear God, thank you for giving us our wonderful family. Help us to always show our love for one another.*

# God Chooses Mary

A new boy moved in next door. He did not know anyone.

Tina's mom said, "I think he could use a friend. Will you say hello to him?"

Tina thought about it. She knew it would make the boy happy. She said yes.

When have you done something to make someone else happy?

## Prayer

*Jesus, help me say yes to God. I want to love God as Mary did.*

# God Loves Mary

God chose Mary to be Jesus' mother.

Mary said she wanted to serve God.

Mary said yes to God.

God gave Mary the gift of **grace.**
Grace makes us beautiful to God.

Yes!

### 📖 Reading God's Word

*Mary said, "God is happy with me. Everyone will call me blessed."* adapted from Luke 1:48

# The Mother of God

Mary was the first one to know Jesus was coming. She loved him very much. Mary loves us too. We call her the Mother of God.

### Link to Liturgy

Many Catholic churches have a statue of Mary. Can you find one in your church?

GO TO PAGE 226

## Prayer for Mary

Mary is important to our Church. We have a special prayer for her.

### Hail Mary

*Hail Mary, full of grace,*
*the Lord is with you.*
*Blessed are you among women,*
*and blessed is the fruit*
*of your womb, Jesus.*
*Holy Mary, Mother of God,*
*pray for us sinners,*
*now and at the hour of our death.*
*Amen.*

Now think about these words. Tell Mary you are glad she said yes to God.

# Mary Answers God

What did Mary say to God?

Color the pieces marked with a **Y.**

# Faith Summary

God chose Mary to be the mother of Jesus. Mary said yes to God.

## Word I Learned

grace

## Ways of Being Like Jesus

Jesus loves his mother, Mary. *Say yes to God and to your family. Show your love for them.*

## Prayer

*Jesus, Son of Mary, thank you for helping me to grow in grace. I will say yes to God each day.*

## With My Family

**Activity** Who are some special women in your family? Mom? Grandma? An aunt? Do something nice for them to show your love.

**Faith on the Go** Ask one another: *How can you show grace to your family?*

**Family Prayer** *Dear God, thank you for the gift of grace. Help us to remember to see God's grace in others.*

# Celebrating Christmas

**Christmas** is celebrated on December 25. The season of Christmas lasts from Christmas Eve, December 24, until the Feast of the Baptism of Jesus.

## Prayer

*Dear Jesus, I know you will be with me during the Christmas season.*

# We Celebrate During Christmas

Christmas is a time to celebrate the birth of Jesus. He is the **Son of God** who came to save us.

How do you celebrate the birth of Jesus?

### Son of God Word Search

Find and circle the words from the word box.

| Jesus | Christmas | God | save |
|-------|-----------|-----|------|

| | | | | | | | |
|---|---|---|---|---|---|---|---|
| F | H | C | E | P | G | O | D |
| V | U | H | A | I | T | H | F |
| A | C | R | R | J | M | Y | B |
| J | I | I | M | I | E | R | U |
| E | R | S | A | I | S | E | R |
| S | O | T | L | E | S | N | U |
| U | A | M | B | O | I | I | L |
| S | A | A | K | S | A | V | E |
| N | D | S | U | F | T | B | A |

### Reading God's Word

Truly you are the Son of God.

*adapted from Matthew 14:33*

# Mass During Christmas

When you go to Mass during Christmas, the church will be decorated with trees, wreaths, and lights.

## What We Experience

When you look around your church, you may see many colors. During the Christmas season the **celebrant** wears white vestments. We sing joyful songs about Jesus' birth.

### My Christmas Tree

Decorate the Christmas tree with ornaments and lights.

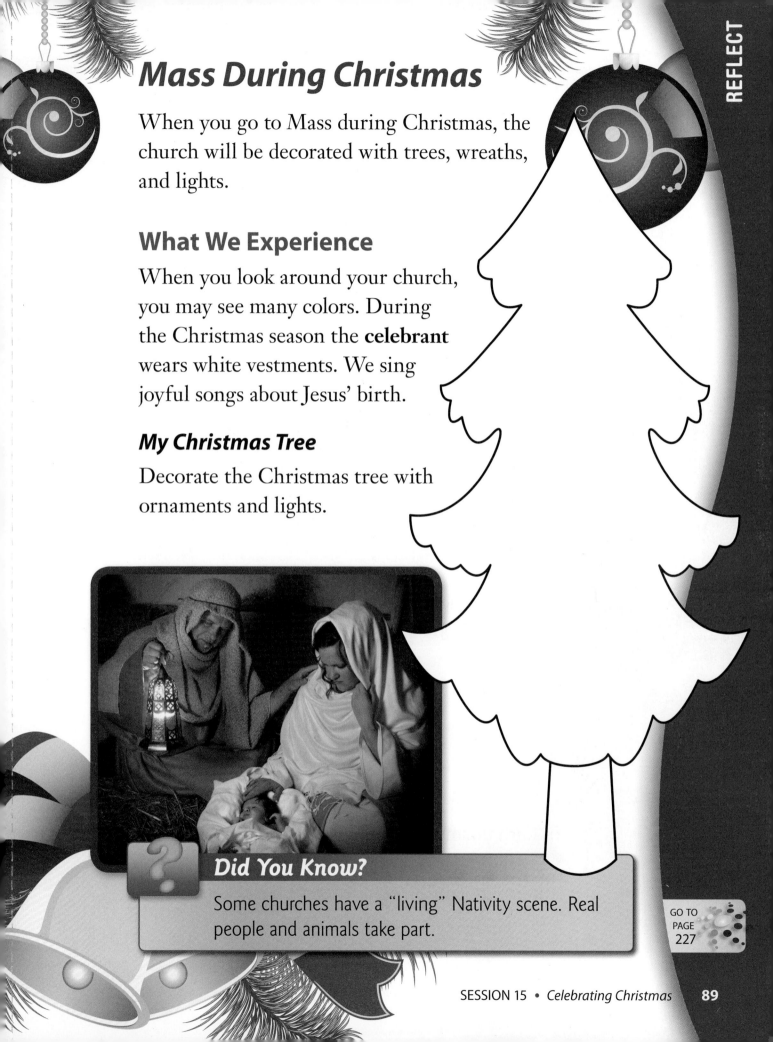

### ? Did You Know?

Some churches have a "living" Nativity scene. Real people and animals take part.

GO TO PAGE 227

# Faith Summary

Christmas is a time to celebrate the birth of Jesus. Jesus is the Son of God who came to save us.

| Words I Learned | Ways of Being Like Jesus |
|---|---|
| celebrant | Jesus brought joy to the world. |
| Christmas | *Share your joy this Christmas.* |
| Son of God | *Sing a Christmas carol to remind others of Jesus' birth.* |

## Prayer

*Dear Jesus, thank you for the gift of the season of Christmas. Help me to remember that you are the reason we celebrate this special season.*

## With My Family

**Activity** When you go to Mass during Christmas, look around your church. Find examples of the things described on page 89. Talk about what you see.

**Faith on the Go** Ask one another: *What is your favorite Christmas tradition?*

**Family Prayer** Invite family members to grow in faith during Christmas. Join hands when you say grace before dinner. End the meal by asking one family member to read the Nativity story from Luke 2:1–19 or Matthew 2:1–12.

# Sacraments, Our Way of Life

## Saint Thérèse of the Child Jesus

Saint Thérèse loved God. She wanted to do everything for him. She said yes to God every day.

## Saint Thérèse of the Child Jesus

Thérèse became a saint by doing her best all the time. She loved God very much. When Thérèse was 15 years old, she became a Carmelite sister and dedicated her life to God. Thérèse wanted to do little things for God every day. She called this her "Little Way."

We can be like Thérèse too. We can always do our best. We can do little things for God every day.

**Saint Thérèse**

Lola cares for Dad. She helps him cook dinner.

What other signs do we use to show our love?

# Jesus in Our Lives

### Prayer

*Jesus, my friend, help me see the signs of your love. Then I will know you are near.*

# Jesus Loves Us

Jesus gives us signs of his love. We call these signs **sacraments**.

Sacraments give us God's grace. They help us live the way God wants us to live. Sacraments bring us closer to Jesus.

## Did You Know?

Jesus gave us the sacraments.

# Caring for Our Spirit

**Priests** are men who accept God's special call to serve the Church. They share signs of Jesus' love. They guide our Church. Priests help us celebrate the sacraments.

Circle the priest in each picture.

### Reading God's Word

Enjoy God's goodness. Let him protect you. Then you will be happy.

*adapted from Psalm 34:9*

GO TO PAGE 228

## Being with Jesus

Imagine that you are sitting next to Jesus. He puts his hand on your forehead. He blesses you. He smiles at you. He takes time with you.

Jesus wants you to know that you are special. How does knowing that make you feel? What will you say to Jesus? Will you tell him you love him? Will you thank him? Be still with Jesus. Enjoy being with him.

# Special Time with Jesus

Jesus loves you very much. He loves when you spend time talking with him and sharing what is in your heart.

Draw a picture of you and Jesus. Then write Jesus a note telling him how much you love him.

Dear Jesus,_____

_____

_____

_____

# Faith Summary

Jesus gives us signs of his love. We call them sacraments. Sacraments help us live the way God wants us to live.

## Words I Learned

**priest**

**sacrament**

## Ways of Being Like Jesus

Jesus shows us that he loves us. *Show signs of your love. Let someone else go first when you play.*

### Prayer

*Dear Jesus, thank you for showing me signs that you are near.*

## With My Family

**Activity** Show a brother, sister, or family member a sign of your love. Play nicely with him or her.

**Faith on the Go** Ask one another: *In what little ways can you show your love every day?*

**Family Prayer** *Dear God, thank you for the gifts of your sacraments. Be with us as we share signs of our love every day.*

How do you use water? How does it taste when you are thirsty? How does it feel on a hot day?

Water is special. It brings life to plants and animals. It brings life to us too.

# Joining God's Family

### Prayer

*Jesus, my brother, teach me that I am part of God's family.*

# Our First Sacrament

**Baptism** is a sacrament. It is the first sacrament we receive. Through Baptism we become followers of Jesus.

What happens when we are baptized?

We become adopted children of God.

We become part of God's family.

We receive the Holy Spirit.

Once we were small. A priest poured blessed water on us. Now we are older. Now we can bless ourselves with the Sign of the Cross. We use the blessed water called **holy water.** It reminds us of our Baptism.

# Godparents Are Special People

Special people come to our Baptism. We call them **godparents.** They help our parents.

How do godparents help? They help teach us about God. They help us lead good lives.

### Reading God's Word

Teach everyone about me. Baptize them in the name of the Father, and of the Son, and of the Holy Spirit.

*adapted from Matthew 28:19*

GO TO PAGE 229

## Being Part of God's Family

Remember that God our Father creates you. Jesus his Son loves you. The Holy Spirit gives you the gift of peace.

You were welcomed into God's family when you were baptized. You can show that you are part of his family. You can pray the Sign of the Cross.

*In the name of the Father,*
*and of the Son,*
*and of the Holy Spirit.*
*Amen.*

# What Is the Word?

Match each sentence to the correct picture.
Write the number in the box.

**1.** These people help us learn about God.

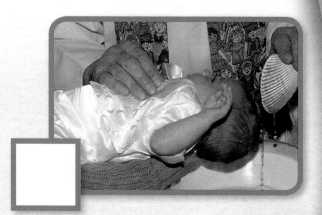

**2.** We become followers of Jesus with this sacrament.

**3.** We use this to remind us of our Baptism.

 **Did You Know?**

Every Catholic church has holy water. Where is holy water in your church?

## Living My Faith

# Faith Summary

In Baptism we become part of God's family. We receive the Holy Spirit.

### Words I Learned

**Baptism**
**godparent**
**holy water**

### Ways of Being Like Jesus

Jesus welcomes us into his family at Baptism. *Thank Jesus that you are a member of the Catholic Church.*

## Prayer

*Jesus, my friend, thank you for the gift of Baptism. Your love makes me special.*

## With My Family

*Activity* Dip your hand in holy water. Pray the Sign of the Cross. Remember you are baptized.

*Faith on the Go* Ask one another: *What's one way you can show God you're thankful for the gift of Baptism?*

*Family Prayer* Dear God, please bless all our godparents. Be with them as they guide our lives.

# Celebrating Jesus

Michael and his family eat together. They share. They pray.

When did you have a special meal? Who was there? Why was it special?

## Prayer

*Jesus, help me know you are always with me.*

# A Special Meal with Jesus

Jesus was with his friends. They were having a meal.

Jesus took bread. He blessed it. He broke it. Then he shared it with his friends. He said, "Eat this. Remember me."

Then Jesus took a cup of wine. He blessed it. He shared it with his friends. He said, "Drink this. I will always be with you."

*adapted from Luke 22:19–20*

# The Last Supper

The meal Jesus shared is called the **Last Supper.** It was a special meal.

We have a special meal. It is called the Mass. Jesus is with us in a special way.

### Link to Liturgy

The priest consecrates the Bread and Wine. The Bread and Wine become Jesus' Body and Blood.

GO TO PAGE 230

**Prayer**

## Mealtime Prayers

### Prayer Before Meals

We pray a special prayer before we eat.
We fold our hands. We think about
all God gives us.

> *Bless us, O Lord, and these your gifts*
> *which we are about to receive from*
> *your goodness.*
> *Through Christ our Lord.*
> *Amen.*

### Prayer After Meals

We pray a special prayer after we eat.
We fold our hands. We think about
how blessed we are.

> *We give you thanks*
> *for all your gifts,*
> *almighty God,*
> *living and reigning*
> *now and for ever.*
> *Amen.*

# My Special Meal

What if you had a special meal? Who would be there? What would you eat?

Finish the picture. Then color it.

## Living My Faith

# Faith Summary

We go to Mass every Sunday. We share a special meal. Jesus is with us in his Body and Blood. The Bread and Wine truly become the Body and Blood of Jesus Christ.

### Words I Learned

**Last Supper**

### Ways of Being Like Jesus

Jesus had a special meal with his friends. *Pray before and after meals. Thank God for all his blessings.*

## Prayer

*Jesus, my friend, thank you for giving yourself to me.*

## With My Family

*Activity*  Help plan a special meal. Assist with cooking, setting the table, or cleaning up.

*Faith on the Go*  Ask one another: *What's your favorite meal to share together?*

*Family Prayer*  Dear God, thank you for the gift of our family. Be with us as we share meals together.

When have you had
a special quiet time?
What did you think about?
How did you feel?

# Listening to Our Father

## Prayer

*Dear Jesus, help me to be still and to listen when I pray.*

# Elijah Listens for God

Elijah loved God. He wanted to be alone with him. So he went to a cave. God said, "Go outside. Listen for me. I will be passing by."

Whoosh! A great wind blew. But Elijah could not hear God. Roar! A loud earthquake shook the ground. Elijah could not hear God. Hiss! A fire lit up the sky. Elijah still could not hear God.

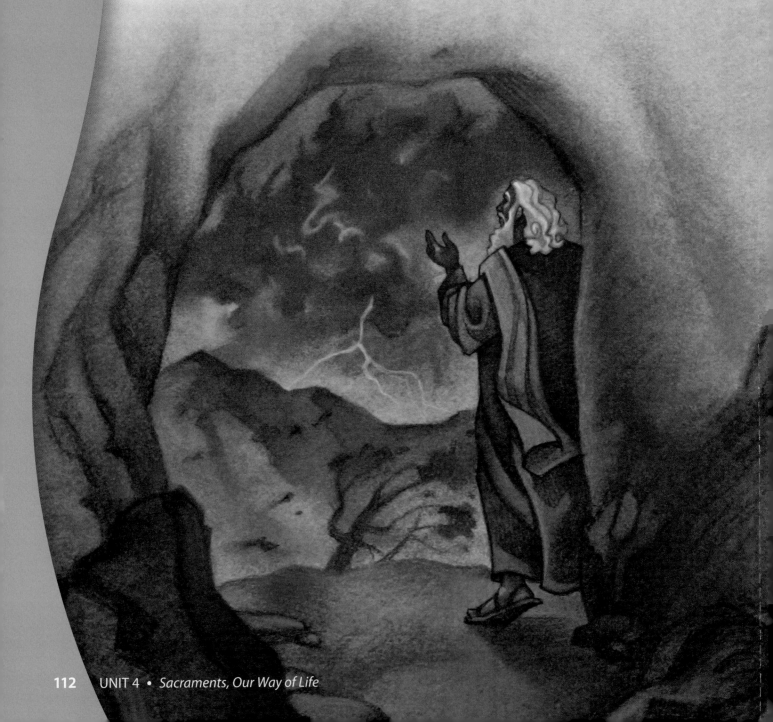

Elijah stood very still. Then he heard something. It was a tiny whisper. He listened closely. It was God talking to him.

*adapted from 1 Kings 19:9–13*

### Reading God's Word

Listen to my Father. Learn from him. Then you will come to me.

*adapted from John 6:45*

GO TO PAGE 231

## Listen for God

Elijah wanted to hear God. Loud sounds filled the air. So he listened closely. Elijah heard a small sound. It was God talking to him.

Think about the sounds you hear every day. What are some small sounds around you? Falling rain? Rustling leaves? Soft whispers?

Now be very quiet, as Elijah was. Listen for God. He is all around you. Tell God you will always listen for what he wants you to know.

# Where Can We Find God?

God is always with us. He is everywhere. God wants us to talk to him. He wants us to listen to him. But we need to be quiet to hear God. This is what Elijah did.

## Quiet Places

Think about quiet places. Which is your favorite? Draw a picture of it.

## Faith Summary

God is everywhere. We may need to listen closely to hear him. We can always pray to him.

### Word I Learned

**gestures***

### Ways of Being Like Jesus

Jesus listened to God Our Father. *Find a quiet time each day to listen to God in your heart.*

### Prayer

*Dear God, thank you for helping me to listen. You are always in my heart.*

## With My Family

*Activity* Make a special, quiet place. It could be near a window, in your bedroom, or in your yard. Go to your special place to pray.

*Faith on the Go* Ask one another: *Where is your favorite place to go when you want quiet time to pray?*

*Family Prayer Dear God, thank you for teaching us to listen for you. Now we know you are everywhere.*

* This word is taught with the Art Print. See page 231.

# Celebrating Lent and Holy Week

The season of **Lent** begins on Ash Wednesday and ends on Holy Thursday evening. It lasts for 40 days.

**Holy Week** is celebrated the week before Easter.

## Prayer

*Dear Jesus, help me to grow closer to you this Lent.*

# Growing Closer to God

Lent is a time to grow closer to God. It is a time to learn to be more like Jesus.

How can you grow closer to God?

_____

How can you be more like Jesus

at school?_____

at home?_____

## Ash Wednesday

On Ash Wednesday the priest traces the Sign of the Cross on our foreheads with ashes.

Finish the Sign of the Cross prayer. Write the correct word from the word box on the line.

> Father        Holy Spirit        Son

*In the name of the* _____,

*and of the* _____,

*and of the* _____.

*Amen.*

### Reading God's Word

Our love for God is showing in our deeds.

*adapted from* 1 John 3:18

# Mass During Lent and Holy Week

You will not hear the **Alleluia** sung at Mass during Lent and Holy Week. The only music that is played is to accompany hymns.

## What We Experience

Look around your church during Lent. You may see plain linens and simple decorations. The priest's vestments are purple. You will not see flowers in the sanctuary.

### My Parish Priest

Color the Lenten vestments. Write your priest's name.

Father _____

**Did You Know?**

Pretzels are a symbol of prayer and penance during Lent.

GO TO PAGE 232

# Faith Summary

During Lent and Holy Week, we learn to be more like Jesus. It is a time to grow closer to God.

| Words I Learned | Ways of Being Like Jesus |
| --- | --- |
| **Alleluia** | Jesus loved others and always |
| **Holy Week** | showed kindness. *Speak kind words.* |
| **Lent** | *Be more patient.* |

## Prayer

*Dear God, thank you for Jesus. Help me to be more like him this Lent.*

## With My Family

*Activity* Look around your church at Mass during Lent and Holy Week. Find examples of the things described on page 119. Talk about what you see.

*Faith on the Go* Ask one another: *How can I be more like Jesus?*

*Family Prayer* Use Lent and Holy Week to invite family members to grow in faith. Take turns leading mealtime prayers. Encourage family members to be thoughtful about their prayers.

# Morality, Our Lived Faith

### Saint Ignatius of Loyola
Saint Ignatius saw God's love everywhere.

# Saint Ignatius

Ignatius was born long ago. He was a brave soldier. He did not think of God often.

One day Ignatius got hurt. As he was healing, he read. He prayed. He learned about God. Slowly Ignatius began to change.

Ignatius made a decision. He chose to live like Jesus. He obeyed God's wishes. He cared for others. He loved his family. He loved God's world. Now God came first in Ignatius's life.

Ignatius became one of God's greatest followers.

# STOP

What is a rule? Why do we have rules? Rules keep us safe. Rules keep us happy. Rules help us live in peace.

# Making Good Decisions

## Prayer

*Jesus, my guide, teach me to do what is right. Then I will be happy.*

## God's Rules

God gives us rules too. We call them **commandments.**

God said, "This is how you can show me your love. Make me important in your life. Use my name in nice ways. Make Sunday a special day."

Then God said, "This is how you can show others your love. Obey your parents. Be kind to everyone. Take only what belongs to you. Tell the truth. Be happy with what you have."

*adapted from Exodus 20:1–17*

# Decisions

Think about the decisions you make.

Do you **decide** to take time to talk to God?

Do you **decide** to be kind to someone?

Do you **decide** to follow school rules?

We make decisions every day. It is not always easy to choose to do the right thing. God will always help us. That is why God gave us commandments.

I can make good decisions.

 **Did You Know?**

God will always help us follow his commandments.

GO TO PAGE 233

## Begin Each Day with Prayer

Each day is a new day. Each day we have new choices. We show God our love when we make good decisions.

**Morning Prayer**

*God, our Father, I offer you today
all that I think and do and say.
I offer it with what was done
on earth by Jesus Christ, your Son.
Amen.*

Think about the commandments God gave us. They help us make good decisions.

Now talk with God about the good decisions you will make today. Ask him to help you be kind.

# What Should You Do?

Read each group of sentences. For a good decision, draw a ☺. For a bad decision, draw a ☹.

Mom asks you to pick up your toys. You do it right away.

You find some money. It is not yours. You take it anyway.

You did not do your homework. Your teacher asks you about it. You tell the truth.

# Faith Summary

God gave us commandments. They help us make good decisions. Good decisions bring us peace.

## Word I Learned

**commandment**

## Ways of Being Like Jesus

Jesus always did what was right. *Treat others as you would like to be treated.*

### Prayer

*Jesus, my friend, thank you for helping me follow the commandments. I will try to make good decisions.*

### With My Family

*Activity* Show your love for your neighbors. Surprise them with flowers or a kind note.

*Faith on the Go* Ask one another: *What's your favorite way to show your love to someone?*

*Family Prayer* Dear God, thank you for giving us your commandments. Help us to always follow them.

Did you ever say something hurtful? Did you ever take something that was not yours? How did you feel? How do you think the other person felt?

# Jesus Cares for Us

## Prayer

*Jesus, my helper, teach me how to care. Then I can help others.*

# *God Always Forgives*

When we choose to do something wrong, we **sin.** A sin can be something we do. A sin can be something we say.

Sins hurt our friendship with God and with others.

## *Avoid Sin*

Read each idea that describes how someone might sin. Then write how you can avoid the sin.

Instead of taking a toy that's not mine, I can _____.

Instead of telling a lie, I can _____ _____.

When we are sorry, we ask God for **forgiveness.** God always forgives us because God's love is greater than any sin.

There are many different ways to say we are sorry. It is important to realize we have made a mistake and to ask for forgiveness.

I want to be your friend.

I will try to do better.

I am sorry.

### Link to Liturgy

At the beginning of Mass, we ask Jesus for forgiveness.

GO TO PAGE 234

## Pray for Forgiveness

Think about the story of the lost sheep. Imagine being that lost sheep. How would you feel? Lonely? Scared? Now imagine a shepherd coming to find you. Think about how happy and safe you feel.

This is how Jesus cares for us. Sometimes we do things that are unkind or wrong. But Jesus always comes to find us. He forgives us.

Think about a time that you did something wrong. Tell Jesus you are sorry. Ask him to forgive you. Listen for what Jesus wants you to know. Jesus will always love you, no matter what.

# A Caring Shepherd

Jesus is like a caring shepherd. He always brings us back to him. He does so as gently as a shepherd carries a little lamb.

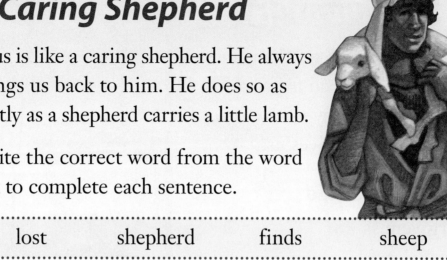

Write the correct word from the word box to complete each sentence.

> lost          shepherd          finds          sheep

1. Jesus is like a _____.

2. We are like his _____.

3. Jesus looks for us when we are _____.

4. He always _____ us.

### Reading God's Word

Jesus said, "I am the good shepherd."      *John 10:11*

# Faith Summary

God's love is greater than any sin. When we feel bad for what we have done, we say we are sorry. God always forgives us.

## Words I Learned

forgiveness

sin

## Ways of Being Like Jesus

Jesus taught us about forgiveness. *When someone says "I'm sorry," say "I forgive you." When you do something wrong, say "I'm sorry."*

## Prayer

*Jesus, thank you for teaching me about forgiveness. Help me to forgive others.*

## With My Family

**Activity** Talk about a time someone forgave you. How did you feel?

**Faith on the Go** Ask one another: *Is it easy or difficult to forgive someone?*

**Family Prayer** *Dear God, thank you for the gift of forgiveness. Help us to forgive others as you always forgive us.*

What are some things your parents ask you to do? Is it ever hard to obey them?

# Jesus Loves Families

### *Prayer*

*Jesus, Son of God, show me how to love and obey my parents.*

# Jesus Obeyed His Parents

Jesus and his parents were at a great celebration. On the way home, Mary and Joseph saw that Jesus was not with them. They were very worried. So they rushed back.

Mary and Joseph looked for Jesus. Finally they found him. Mary said to Jesus, "We have been worried about you."

Mary and Joseph told Jesus, "Now come home with us." Jesus did as his parents said.

*adapted from Luke 2:41–51*

# A Special Gift

God gave your parents a gift. He gave them YOU.

Your parents were happy, and they took good care of you. Your parents made sure you were warm. They made sure you were fed. They taught you about God.

You **honor** and thank your parents when you **obey** them.

GO TO PAGE 235

## A Prayer to End Each Day

At the end of each day, we think about what we have done. We think about the decisions we made. We think about how we showed God our love.

### Evening Prayer

*God, our Father, this day is done. We ask you and Jesus Christ, your Son, that with the Spirit, our welcome guest, you guard our sleep and bless our rest. Amen.*

Now think about your family. Tell God how much you love them. Ask God to bless them.

# Show You Care

How can you show your parents that you care? Find and circle the words shown in the word box.

| honor | love | obey | help |
|-------|------|------|------|

**Chore List**

Set table

Fold clothes

Feed the dog

Take out the garbage

| Z | L | Q | P | L | V |
|---|---|---|---|---|---|
| H | O | N | O | R | Z |
| W | V | Q | B | R | I |
| X | E | H | E | L | P |
| K | I | B | Y | Q | W |

We love you, Mom and Dad.

### Reading God's Word

Love your mother and father. Obey them. Help them. Then you will have a long and happy life.

*adapted from Exodus 20:12*

## Living My Faith

# Faith Summary

Jesus loved and obeyed his parents. God wants us to obey our parents too. When we show love for our parents, we show love for God.

## Words I Learned

honor

obey

## Ways of Being Like Jesus

Jesus honored his parents. *Show your parents that you love and honor them. Obey them and be polite.*

### Prayer

*Jesus, Son of God, thank you for teaching me to obey and care for my parents.*

## With My Family

*Activity* Talk with your parents about when they were young. What kinds of rules did they have to obey?

*Faith on the Go* Ask one another: *Which rule is the hardest for you to follow?*

*Family Prayer* Dear God, thank you for the gift of our family. Help us to better listen to one another and love more each day.

How can you show that you care about God's creation?

# God Loves the World

### Prayer

*Jesus, help me take care of God's world. Then I can show my love for all of creation.*

# Caring for Our World

God made our world. That is why it is beautiful. We help keep it beautiful. We take care of the animals and plants. We do this for ourselves. We do this for our **neighbors.** We do this for God.

### Did You Know?

Forests are special places. They give animals homes. They keep our air clean. They even give us important medicines.

# Caring for God's Creatures

Matt and Kara were playing by a pond when Matt saw something move. "What is it?" asked Matt. It was a small, scared turtle. They ran to Mom and Dad and asked, "Can we keep it?"

"No," they replied. Dad said this was a healthy turtle. "God made special homes for these turtles. We have to care for God's world."

Dad gently placed the turtle by the water. Plop! Into the water it crawled and swam away.

Everyone smiled. "God's world is a beautiful place," said Dad.

GO TO PAGE 236

## A Nature Prayer

Imagine you are outside. It is your favorite kind of day. Maybe you see clouds. Maybe you feel a gentle breeze. Look around. Maybe you see your favorite animals too. You can see all of your favorite things that God created.

God loves us. He fills our lives with beautiful things. Thank God for these things. Tell him how you will care for them. Listen in your heart to what God wants you to know.

# What Can You Do?

How will you care for God's world?
Draw a picture and write a sentence.

_____

_____

## Link to Liturgy

At the end of Mass, we go in peace to show our love for God and all of creation.

# Faith Summary

God made a beautiful world. He wants us to care for plants and animals. We take care of them for ourselves and others.

## Word I Learned

neighbor

## Ways of Being Like Jesus

Jesus cared for the gifts God gave him. *Care for God's world. Be kind to every living thing.*

### Prayer

*Thank you, God, for this beautiful world. I will care for the wonderful things you have given me.*

### With My Family

*Activity* Talk with your family about making your porch or yard animal-friendly. Can you make and hang a birdhouse or a bird feeder?

*Faith on the Go* Ask one another: *What's one thing you can do every day to take care of our beautiful world?*

*Family Prayer* Dear God, we are so grateful for your gift of this beautiful world. Guide our steps every day to help us respect and protect all you've created.

# Celebrating Easter

**Easter** is celebrated on the first Sunday after the first full moon of spring. The Easter season begins with the Easter Vigil and continues for the next 50 days.

### Prayer

*Dear Jesus, help me to love and show kindness.*

## We Celebrate During Easter

Easter is a time to celebrate how Jesus saves us all. We are glad because God the Father raised Jesus Christ from the dead.

Jesus died on the cross for me.

Jesus is with me always.

God's love is so great to send his only Son for me.

Use the key to color the picture below. Then read the hidden word.

1 – blue     2 – green     3 – pink     4 – yellow

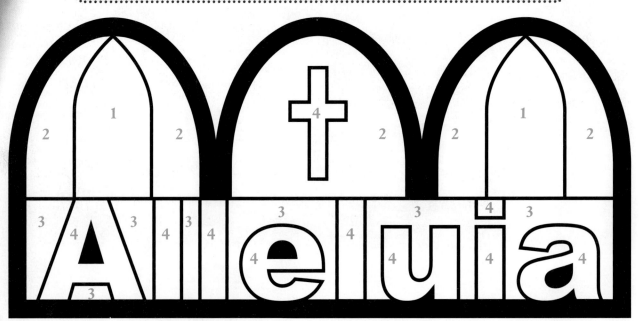

### Reading God's Word

Jesus came to see his friends. He said, "Peace be with you."     *adapted from Luke 24:36*

# Mass During Easter

When you go to Mass during the Easter season, you will hear people singing and praying "Alleluia!" We are happy because Jesus promised to be with us always.

## What We Experience

When you look around your church, you may see symbols of Easter. One symbol is the Easter lily. Notice the color of the priest's vestments. Are they white or gold?

Many churches are decorated with flowers for the Easter season.

Color the lily. Write the name of a person you will pray for this Easter season.

I will pray for _____.

### Did You Know?

Every year the White House hosts an Easter egg roll.

GO TO PAGE 237

# Faith Summary

At Easter, we celebrate God the Father raising Jesus from the dead to save us all from sin and death.

## Word I Learned

**Easter**

## Ways of Being Like Jesus

Jesus gave us the gift of himself. *Give of yourself to others. Help out with a baby brother or sister.*

## Prayer

Dear Jesus, fill my heart with joy and love.

## With My Family

*Activity* When you go to Mass during the Easter season, look around your church. Find examples of the things described on page 149. Talk about what you see.

*Faith on the Go* Ask one another: *What is one way you will celebrate Easter?*

*Family Prayer* Use Easter to invite family members to grow by praying together. Each day ask Jesus, the risen Christ, to help you give of yourself to others.

# The Year in Our Church

The liturgical calendar shows us the feasts and seasons of the Church year.

Christmas

Ordinary Time

Lent

Holy Week

Epiphany

Ash Wednesday

Palm Sunday
Holy Thursday
Good Friday
Holy Saturday

Christmas

Easter Sunday

Easter

Advent

Winter

Spring

Fall

Summer

First Sunday
of Advent

Ascension
Pentecost

All Souls Day
All Saints Day

Ordinary Time

## Liturgical Year

During **Advent** we get ready to welcome Jesus.

**Christmas** celebrates the time when Jesus was born.

**Lent** is the time before Easter. It is a time to learn to be more like Jesus.

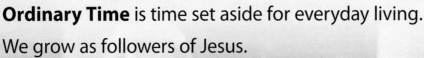

**Holy Week** is the week before Easter. We remember that Jesus died for us.

On **Easter** Jesus rose from the dead.

On **Pentecost** the Holy Spirit came to Jesus' friends.

**All Saints Day** is the day we remember everyone in Heaven.

**Ordinary Time** is time set aside for everyday living. We grow as followers of Jesus.

# Advent

Mary and Joseph waited for Jesus to be born. We wait to celebrate Jesus' birth. We call this time of waiting Advent.

**Prayer**

*God, help me be patient as I prepare for Christmas.*

# Waiting for Jesus

Jesus was about to be born. Mary and Joseph were getting ready for him.

But their ruler wanted to count all his people. So Mary and Joseph went to be counted. They had to go far from home. They had nowhere to rest. So they stayed in a stable. They waited there for Jesus to be born.

*adapted from Luke 2:1–7*

## What Did Mary and Joseph Do?

Unscramble the letters. Then write them in the blanks.

w t a i d e

Mary and Joseph

_ _ _ _ _ _

for Jesus.

# The Advent Wreath

Did you ever have to wait for something? Sometimes it is hard to wait. But our wait can be worth it!

The Advent wreath reminds us we are waiting to celebrate the birth of Jesus. It reminds us Jesus is coming.

The Advent wreath has four candles. Usually three of the candles are purple and one is pink. We light a candle each week. Each lit candle means Christmas is getting closer.

Write how you will celebrate Advent.

I will _____

_____

_____

_____.

**Leader:** *Jesus is the light of the world.*

*A reading from the Book of Isaiah.*

Rise up! God's light shines upon you. The earth is dark, and it is hard to see, but God will light the way.

*adapted from Isaiah 60:1–2*

*The Word of the Lord.*

**All:** *Thanks be to God.*

**Leader:** *Dear God, help us to be children of the light. Guide us as we prepare for the coming of Jesus.*

**All:** *Come, Lord Jesus.*

# Christmas

Shepherds were watching their sheep. An angel came to them. The shepherds were afraid. The angel said, "Do not be afraid. I have good news. Jesus has been born."

Then more angels came. They said, "Glory to God. Peace on earth."

*adapted from Luke 2:8–14*

**Prayer**

*Thank you, God, for sending us your Son, Jesus.*

# Looking for Jesus

The shepherds were very happy. They went to find Jesus.

*adapted from Luke 2:15*

## God's Gift to Everyone

God sent Jesus to Mary and Joseph. God sent Jesus to the shepherds. God sent Jesus to us. Jesus is a gift to all of us.

# Good News

The shepherds heard the good news. Jesus, the Prince of Peace, was born. We can be like Jesus. We can help one another live in peace. We can obey our parents. We can be nice to our brothers and sisters.

Help the shepherds find Jesus.

**Leader:** *Blessed be God.*

**All:** *Now and forever.*

**Leader:** *We celebrate the good news of Jesus' birth. Let us welcome him into our lives. Let us live in peace together.*

*A reading from the Book of Isaiah.*

A child is born for us. A son is given to us. They call him Mighty God. They call him Prince of Peace. He will rule in peace forever.

*adapted from Isaiah 9:5–6*

*The Word of the Lord.*

**All:** *Thanks be to God.*

# Lent

Lent is a special time of year. It is a time to grow closer to God.

### Prayer

*Jesus, my guide, help me to do good things this Lent.*
*I want to stay close to God.*

# Grow with God

This tree grows near a stream. It is healthy. The water from the stream nourishes it. The water helps it grow strong.

We are like the healthy tree. God is like our stream. When we are close to him, we grow stronger and happier.

*adapted from Psalm 1:3*

## A Special Time

The first day of Lent is called Ash Wednesday. The priest places ashes on our foreheads. The ashes remind us that Lent is a special time.

During Lent we make a special effort to do good deeds. We try to be more like Jesus. Then we can grow closer to God. What good deeds will you do during Lent? Write about it on the leaves.

I will

_____

_____

_____.

I will

_____

_____

_____.

I will

_____

_____

_____.

**Leader:** *Let us begin our prayer with the Sign of the Cross.*

*We offer God our good deeds in this time of Lent. Let us pray that they will help us grow closer to God.*

*A reading from the holy Gospel according to John.*

> I am the vine, and you are the branches. If you stay close to me and I to you, you will produce much fruit.
>
> *adapted from John 15:5*

*The Gospel of the Lord.*

**All:** *Praise to you, Lord Jesus Christ.*

# Holy Week

During Holy Week we think about how Jesus lived. Jesus taught his friends to love others. How do you show others your love?

**Prayer**

*Jesus, my teacher, help me show my love to others.*

*I want to be like you.*

# Jesus Teaches His Friends

Jesus loved his friends very much. He wanted them to know this. Jesus decided to show them. So he put some water in a bowl. Then Jesus washed his friends' feet.

Jesus said, "You say that I am your teacher. If I am, learn from me. I am your friend. If I wash your feet, you should wash the feet of others. Treat others as I treat you." *adapted from John 13:1–15*

## Love One Another

Jesus showed his friends how to love others. He wanted them to do as he did. Jesus wants us to follow his example too. When we help others, we are being like Jesus.

You can follow in Jesus' footsteps. You can show others your love. What can you do? Finish the sentence.

I can be like Jesus.
I can _____
_____.

**Leader:** *Jesus was sad to leave his friends. Before he left, he gave them a special message.*

*A reading from the holy Gospel according to John.*

My children, I will be with you only a little while longer. Then I will be gone. I give you a new commandment: love one another. You should love one another as I have loved you. Then everyone will know you are my friends.

*adapted from John 13:33–35*

*The Gospel of the Lord.*

**All:** *Praise to you, Lord Jesus Christ.*

**Leader:** *Let us always remember to walk in the footsteps of Jesus.*

**All:** *In the name of the Father,*

*and of the Son,*

*and of the Holy Spirit.*

*Amen.*

# Easter

Easter is a happy time. We celebrate Jesus Christ's rising from the dead. His Resurrection fills us with joy.

## Prayer

*Jesus, my friend, help me follow you. I want to be with you someday.*

# Looking for Jesus

Jesus had died. Some women visited his tomb. They saw that the stone was rolled back. The tomb was empty! Then two angels came. The angels said, "Jesus is not here. He has risen." The women were filled with joy. Jesus Christ was alive! The women ran to tell their friends.          *adapted from Luke 24:1–9*

## Jesus Appeared to Many

On their way the women saw Jesus. Many more people saw him too. After Jesus saw his friends, it was time for him to leave. Jesus went to Heaven. He went to be with God, his Father.

# The Lord's Day

Why is Sunday special? It is the day we celebrate Jesus' Resurrection. It is the Lord's Day. We celebrate by going to Mass.

In what order did these happen? Use numbers.

The women tell their friends that Jesus is alive.

The women visit the tomb.

The tomb is empty.

The women see angels.

## Prayer Service

**Leader:** *May the grace of Jesus Christ be with us all, now and forever.*

**All:** *Amen.*

**Leader:** *Jesus died and rose from the dead. He gave us new life. On Sundays we remember Jesus Christ's Resurrection.*

**Group A:** This is the day the Lord has made.

**Group B:** Let us rejoice and be glad.

*adapted from Psalm 118:24*

**All:** *Alleluia! Alleluia! Alleluia!*

# Pentecost

After Jesus rose from the dead, the Holy Spirit came. It was a time of joy. We call this special time Pentecost.

## Prayer

*Dear Jesus, give me the help of the Holy Spirit. He will help me tell others about you.*

# Sharing Jesus

Philip was a follower of Jesus'. One day Philip went on a trip. On the road he met a man. The man wanted to learn about God.

The Holy Spirit was in Philip's heart. The Holy Spirit said to Philip, "Help the man. Teach the man." So Philip did. He told the man about Jesus.

The man was very happy. He asked Philip, "Will you baptize me?" The man wanted to become part of God's family.

*adapted from Acts of the Apostles 8:26–38*

## The Holy Spirit Is with Us

The Holy Spirit was with Philip. The Holy Spirit is with all of us too. We can celebrate Pentecost every day. We can help others know Jesus. We can do this by telling them about Jesus. The Holy Spirit will help us.

Show that the Holy Spirit is with you. Write your name on the line. Then show how you can help someone. Draw a picture in the dove.

The Holy Spirit is with _____.

**Prayer Service**

**Leader:** *Jesus wants us all to share what we know about him. Let us listen to what he told his followers.*

*A reading from the Acts of the Apostles.*

The Holy Spirit will come upon you.

He will make you strong.

He will help you tell people all over the world about me.

*adapted from Acts of the Apostles 1:8*

*The Word of the Lord.*

**All:** *Thanks be to God.*

# All Saints Day

On All Saints Day, we think of everyone in Heaven.
They are with God. They are saints.

Saint Kateri Tekakwitha

Saint Francis of Assisi

Saint Ignatius

Saint Joseph

Saint Thérèse of Lisieux

Saint Martin de Porres

## Prayer

*Dear God, help me to be like the saints. I want to love you as they did.*

## A Special Day

Think about your birthday. It is a day all for you. It is a day when people show how much they love you.

Saints have a special day too. We call it All Saints Day. On this day we show the saints our love. How? We think about them. We ask them to pray for us.

## Saints Pray for Us

Saints are God's special friends. They are close to him. We ask the saints for their help. We ask them to talk to God for us. The saints ask God to watch over us. The saints ask God to care for us.

Saint Martin de Porres

# Children of God

Our Father loves us very much. We are called the children of God. One day we shall see him. *adapted from 1 John 3:1–2*

Ask someone in Heaven to pray for you. Put your prayer in a special place.

Dear _____,

pray for me. Help me to _____

_____.

Dear _____,

pray for me. Help me to _____

_____.

Dear _____,

pray for me. Help me to _____

_____.

Dear _____,

pray for me. Help me to _____

_____.

**Leader:** *Let us pray to God and thank him for our friends the saints.*

**All:** *We praise you, we bless you, we thank you.*

**Group A:** *Let us give glory to God.*

**Group B:** *Let us praise God's name.*

**All:** *Glory be to the Father,*

*and to the Son,*

*and to the Holy Spirit.*

*As it was in the beginning,*

*is now, and ever shall be,*

*world without end.*

*Amen.*

# Prayers and Practices of Our Faith

# Knowing and Praying Our Faith

## The Bible and You

God speaks to us in many ways. One way is through the Bible.

The Bible is God's message. The Bible is the story of God's promise to care for us. It teaches us about God's love for us.

The Bible teaches us about Jesus. Stories about Jesus are in the Gospels. We can learn about what Jesus said and did.

At Mass we hear stories from the Bible. We learn how we can share God's love with others.

The Bible has two parts. One part is the Old Testament. The other part is the New Testament. In the New Testament, we learn about Jesus.

## Prayer and How We Pray

Prayer is talking to and listening to God.

God is everywhere. We can pray to God at any time and in any place.

God hears our prayers even when we pray silently. We can pray in our own words. We can learn prayers. Sometimes we can just be quiet and enjoy being with God.

We pray to God often and in different ways. We can praise God. We can ask God for what we need. We can thank him. We can pray for ourselves and for others.

Sometimes we pray alone. Other times we pray with others.

God, thank you for loving me.

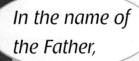

## Prayers to Take to Heart

It is good for us to know prayers by heart. To take prayers to heart means that we not only learn, or memorize, the words but understand and live them.

**Sign of the Cross**

**1**  *In the name of the Father,*

**2**  *and of the Son,*

**3**  *and of the Holy*

**4**  *Spirit.*

**5**  *Amen.*

## Glory Be to the Father

Glory be to the Father,
and to the Son,
and to the Holy Spirit.
As it was in the beginning,
is now, and ever shall be,
world without end.
Amen.

## Lord's Prayer

Our Father, who art in heaven,
hallowed be thy name;
thy kingdom come,
thy will be done
on earth as it is in heaven.
Give us this day our daily bread,
and forgive us our trespasses,
as we forgive those who trespass against us;
and lead us not into temptation,
but deliver us from evil.
Amen.

**Hail Mary**

*Hail Mary, full of grace,*
*the Lord is with you. Blessed are you*
*among women,*
*and blessed is the fruit of your*
*womb, Jesus.*
*Holy Mary, Mother of God,*
*pray for us sinners,*
*now and at the hour of our death.*
*Amen.*

# Praying the Rosary

The Rosary helps us to reflect on the special events, or mysteries, in the lives of Jesus and Mary.

**9.** Pray ten Hail Marys and one Glory Be to the Father.

**10.** Think about the fourth mystery. Pray the Lord's Prayer.

**8.** Think about the third mystery. Pray the Lord's Prayer.

**11.** Pray ten Hail Marys and one Glory Be to the Father.

**7.** Pray ten Hail Marys and one Glory Be to the Father.

**6.** Think about the second mystery. Pray the Lord's Prayer.

**12.** Think about the fifth mystery. Pray the Lord's Prayer.

**5.** Pray ten Hail Marys and one Glory Be to the Father.

**13.** Pray ten Hail Marys and one Glory Be to the Father.

**4.** Think about the first mystery. Pray the Lord's Prayer.

*Pray the Hail, Holy Queen.*
Many people pray the Hail, Holy Queen after the last decade.

**3.** Pray three Hail Marys and one Glory Be to the Father.

**2.** Pray the Lord's Prayer.

**14.** Pray the Sign of the Cross.

**1.** Pray the Sign of the Cross and the Apostles' Creed.

### Guardian Angel Prayer

*Angel of God, my guardian dear,*
*to whom God's love commits me here,*
*ever this day be at my side,*
*to light and guard, to rule and guide.*
*Amen.*

### Prayer for Vocations

*God, thank you for loving me.*
*You have called me*
*to live as your child.*
*Help all your children*
*to love you and one another.*
*Amen.*

### Morning Prayer

*God, our Father, I offer you today*
*all that I think and do and say.*
*I offer it with what was done on earth*
*By Jesus Christ, your Son.*
*Amen.*

### Evening Prayer

*God, our Father, this day is done.*
*We ask you and Jesus Christ, your Son,*
*that with the Spirit, our welcome guest,*
*you guard our sleep and bless our rest.*
*Amen.*

### Prayer Before Meals

*Bless us, O Lord, and these your gifts*
*which we are about to receive from your goodness.*
*Through Christ our Lord.*
*Amen.*

### Prayer After Meals

*We give you thanks*
*for all your gifts,*
*almighty God,*
*living and reigning*
*now and for ever.*
*Amen.*

# Celebrating Our Faith

## The Seven Sacraments

A sacrament is a special sign. Sacraments give us grace.
They show us that Jesus loves us.

Sacraments help us to live the way God wants us to live.
Sacraments are celebrated with us by priests.

### Baptism

Baptism is the first sacrament we
receive. At Baptism a priest pours
blessed water on us. We become
part of God's family, the Church.

## Confirmation

At Confirmation the Holy Spirit makes us stronger in faith. The Holy Spirit helps us become better Christians.

## Eucharist

At Mass the Bread and Wine become Jesus' Body and Blood. The Eucharist is a special meal that Jesus shares with us.

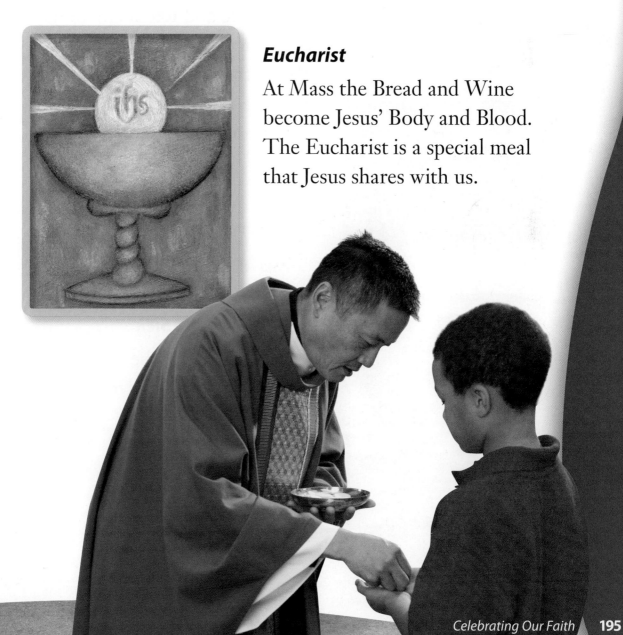

## Penance and Reconciliation

In Penance and Reconciliation we celebrate God's forgiveness. We say that we are sorry for our sins. The priest tells us that God forgives us.

## Anointing of the Sick

The Anointing of the Sick brings Jesus' strength to people who are sick.

## Holy Orders

Some men are called to be deacons, priests, or bishops. They receive the Sacrament of Holy Orders. They do Jesus' work in a special way.

## Matrimony

Some men and women are called to be married. They promise to be faithful to each other for life. They share God's love with their children.

# People and Things I See at Mass

alb

altar server

sanctuary lamp

processional cross

Paschal Candle

tabernacle

ambo

altar servers

extraordinary minister of Holy Communion

stole

chasuble

deacon

priest

lector

cantor

altar

chalice

paten

199

# Living Our Faith

## The Ten Commandments

Rules keep us safe. Rules help us to live in peace. God gives us rules too. We call them the Ten Commandments. We show our love for God by following the commandments.

1. I am your God; love nothing more than me.
2. Use God's name with respect.
3. Keep the Lord's Day holy.
4. Honor and obey your parents.
5. Treat all human life with respect.

I love you, God!

# I'm happy with what I have.

6. Respect married life.
7. Respect what belongs to others.
8. Tell the truth.
9. Respect your neighbors and your friends.
10. Be happy with what you have.

## The Great Commandment

People asked Jesus, "What is the most important commandment?"
Jesus said, "First, love God. Love him with your heart, soul, and
mind. The second is like it: Love your neighbor as yourself."

*adapted from Matthew 22:37–39*

We call this the Great Commandment.

## Showing Our Love for the World

Jesus taught us to care for those in need. The Church teaches us how to do this.

### Life and Dignity

God wants us to care for everyone. We are all made in God's image.

### Family and Community

Jesus wants us to be loving helpers in our families and communities.

### Rights and Responsibilities

All people should have what they need to live good lives.

### The Poor and Vulnerable

Jesus calls us to do what we can to help people in need.

### Work and Workers

The work that we do gives glory to God.

## Solidarity

Since God is our Father, we are called to treat everyone in the world as a brother or a sister.

## God's Creation

We show our love for God's world by taking care of it.

# Songs of Our Faith

## Song of Love

### Chorus

Thank you, Jesus, for helping me to see.
Thank you, God, for the heart you've given me.
Thank you, Spirit, for coming to me,
and for showing me how to sing your song of love.

### Verse 1

I saw someone lonely by the road,
someone my age sadly all alone.
I shared my friendship, and we talked a while.
I gave my hand. Jesus gave back a smile.

### (Sing Chorus)

### Verse 2

I saw Jesus inside my heart,
making me God's own work of art.
If I spread my joy in life each day,
I can show my love for God's world in every way.

### Verse 3

I saw Jesus in friends and family
by my side, sharing and supporting me.
I found my heart had room for everyone.
Thank you, Spirit, for what you have begun.

### (Sing Chorus)

*Lyrics by E. Strauss. Music by Neilson Hubbard.*

# God Is So Good

### Verse 1

God is so good,
God is so good,
God is so good, he's so good to me.

### Verse 2

God loves me so,
God loves me so,
God loves me so, he's so good to me.

### Verse 3

God answers prayer,
God answers prayer,
God answers prayer, he's so good to me.

### Verse 4

God is so good,
God is so good,
God is so good, he's so good to me.

*"God Is So Good" from African American folk song.*

## Our Father

Our Father who art in heaven,
hallowed be thy name;
thy kingdom come,
thy will be done
on earth as it is in heaven.
Give us this day our daily bread,
and forgive us our trespasses,
as we forgive those who trespass against us;
and lead us not into temptation,
but deliver us from evil.
Amen.

*"Our Father" tune from traditional chant.*

# This Is the Day

### Verse 1

This is the day,
this is the day that the Lord has made, that the Lord
has made;
we will rejoice,
we will rejoice and be glad in it, and be glad in it.
This is the day that the Lord has made;
we will rejoice and be glad in it.
This is the day,
this is the day that the Lord has made.

### Verse 2

This is the day,
this is the day when he rose again, when he rose again;
we will rejoice,
we will rejoice and be glad in it, and be glad in it.
This is the day when he rose again;
we will rejoice and be glad in it.
This is the day,
this is the day when he rose again.

## Come, O Holy Spirit / Wa Wa Wa Emimimo

### Verse 1

Come, O Holy Spirit, come.
Come, Almighty Spirit, come.
Come, come, come.

### Verse 2

Come, O Holy Spirit, come.
Come, Almighty Spirit, come.
Come, come, come.

### Verse 3

Wa wa wa Emimimo.
Wa wa wa Alagbara.
Wao, wao, wao.

### Verse 4

Wa wa wa Emimimo.
Wa wa wa Alagbara.
Wao, wao, wao.

*"Come, O Holy Spirit / Wa Wa Wa Emimimo" from traditional Nigerian text. English transcription and paraphrase. © 1990, I-to-Loh (World Council of Churches).*

Come, O Holy Spirit, come.

## Come All You People

Come all you people,
come and praise your Maker,
Come all you people,
come and praise your Maker,
Come all you people,
come and praise your Maker,
Come now and worship the Lord.

**(Repeat twice.)**

# Guide My Feet

### Verse 1

Guide my feet while I run this race.
Guide my feet while I run this race.
Guide my feet while I run this race,
for I don't want to run this race in vain!

### Verse 2

I'm your child while I run this race.
I'm your child while I run this race.
I'm your child while I run this race,
for I don't want to run this race in vain!

### Verse 3

Hold my hand while I run this race.
Hold my hand while I run this race.
Hold my hand while I run this race,
for I don't want to run this race in vain!

### Verse 4

Stand by me while I run this race.
Stand by me while I run this race.
Stand by me while I run this race,
for I don't want to run this race in vain!

*"Guide My Feet" from traditional African
American text and tune.*

Name _____    Date _____

*Art Print 1 shows an image of Saint Vincent de Paul helping people in need. What can you do to help others?*

# *Helping Others*

Like Saint Vincent de Paul, we can show love for God by helping others. Some people build homes for those in need. Some people share their food and clothes.

Draw a picture of yourself donating items to a St. Vincent de Paul center.

Name _____    Date _____

*Art Print 2 shows children helping and showing love for one another.*
*What can you do to show God's love today?*

## God's Love

God loves us and cares for
us. That is why he made us.
He made us to be like him.
When we love and take care
of others, we show our love
for God.

Draw a line to correctly complete each sentence. Then read
aloud each sentence. Afterward, write about a time you showed
God's love.

1. On the playground, I  ●

2. When I play a game
   with someone, I  ●

3. When it's time to
   clean up, I  ●

4. If someone is hurt, I  ●

● **a.** get help for him
   or her.

● **b.** take turns calmly
   and fairly.

● **c.** ask someone
   to play.

● **d.** help put away
   everyone's things.

_____

_____

_____

_____

Name _____     Date _____

*Art Print 3 shows Jesus on a donkey being welcomed by a large group of children. Where can you learn even more about Jesus?*

# God Gave Us His Son

God wants us to know about him. God sent his Son, Jesus, to us. Jesus teaches us that God is our Father. He tells us how much God loves us.

> God said, "This is my wonderful Son. I love him so.
> He makes me happy with everything he does."
>
> *adapted from Matthew 3:17*

On one side of Jesus, draw yourself holding his hand. On the other side, draw a friend or family member holding Jesus' hand.

Name _____ Date _____

*Art Print 4 shows four figures holding up a dove, a symbol for peace.*
*What can you do to bring peace?*

# Bring Peace

You can bring peace to the world in many ways. You can
pray for peace. You can even smile for peace. When you smile,
others feel happy and peaceful. They smile too. They pass on
the smiles. Soon, everyone is smiling. Peace is everywhere!

Draw your smiling face. Add hair.
Color your picture.

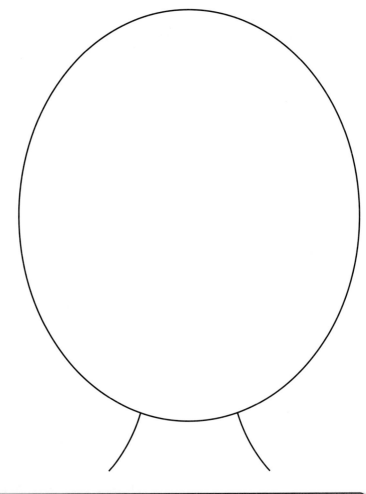

### Reading God's Word

Peace and love be to you from God the Father and his Son, Jesus.

*adapted from Ephesians 6:23*

Name _____ Date _____

*Art Print 5 shows a seedling sprouting from the ground. What can you do to give thanks for God's gifts?*

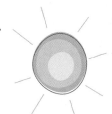

# Celebrating Ordinary Time

Joyful events happen every day of the year. Each morning we wake up to God's love. The sun rises, and plants grow. Members of God's family are thankful for God's creation and for our many gifts. We celebrate everyday miracles during Ordinary Time. We grow closer to God.

Draw a picture of a joyful event that happened to you today. Then write a sentence about it.

_____

_____

_____

Name _____ Date _____

*Art Print 6 shows Jesus in a manger surrounded by Mary, Joseph, and shepherds. What comes to mind when you think of the Nativity?*

# Born in a Stable

Jesus is the Son of God, who became man. He was born in a stable, a shelter for animals such as sheep. Why? God wants to teach us something. He wants us to know that we can find Jesus in unexpected places.

Shepherds were the first to see Jesus. They were everyday people with regular jobs. God wants us to know that Jesus came for all people.

Color the Nativity scene.

### Reading God's Word

Mary kept her feelings in her heart. The shepherds thanked God for all they heard and saw.                    *adapted from Luke 2:19–20*

Name _____ Date _____

*Art Print 7 shows a woman and child picking cherries in an orchard. How can you serve the Kingdom of God?*

## Serving the Kingdom

Because God is our Father and Jesus is his Son, everyone belongs to the **Kingdom of God.** Jesus teaches us about how to serve the Kingdom of God. We can serve the kingdom in many ways.

Read each sentence about how you can serve the Kingdom of God. Then draw a picture for each sentence.

| | |
|---|---|
| Pray for those in need. | Help with a chore at home. |
| Listen to your teacher. | Be kind to animals. |

### Did You Know?

Long ago, grown-ups gave pretzels to children who learned their prayers by heart. Why do you think so?

Name _____    Date _____

*Art Print 8 shows a woman giving a kiss to her child.*
*How do you show someone that you are sorry?*

## Saying We Are Sorry

In the Lord's Prayer, we ask God to help us forgive those who have hurt us. But what can we do when we hurt others? One thing we can do is say, "I'm sorry."

When someone hurts us, we can be like God and forgive that person. We can say, "That's OK. I forgive you."

Write *I'm sorry.* for the child on the left.
Write *That's OK. I forgive you.* for the child on the right.

Name _____  Date _____

*Art Print 9 shows the risen Jesus Christ surrounded by his friends. How can you share the Easter message that Christ is risen?*

# Jesus Is Alive!

Jesus Christ rose from the dead. We call this the **Resurrection.** We celebrate Jesus Christ's Resurrection at Easter.

Jesus' friends remembered all that he taught them. They knew Jesus was with them when they prayed. Jesus is with us, too, when we pray. It's good to know that Jesus is with us always.

Finish each sentence with the correct word from the word box.

> playground     Mass     school     asleep     pray

**Jesus is with me . . .**

1. in the morning when I get ready for _____.

2. when I play with my friends on the _____.

3. when I fold my hands, close my eyes,

   and _____.

4. at night when my eyes are closed and

   I'm _____.

5. when I go to church for _____.

### Link to Liturgy

People around the world celebrate Jesus' Resurrection at Mass.

Name _____    Date _____

*Art Print 10 shows Mary and Joseph's journey to Bethlehem before Jesus' birth. What can you do to welcome Jesus into your heart?*

## Celebrating Advent

The Advent season is the four weeks before Christmas. During that time we prepare to celebrate Jesus' birth. At church we light the candles of the Advent wreath. Each week, one more candle is lit. The light becomes brighter as Jesus' birth nears.

Imagine that Jesus is coming to be a guest in your home. How would you get ready? How would you spend your time with him? Write your sentences below.

_____

_____

_____

_____

_____

_____

_____

_____

Name _____ Date _____

*Art Print 11 shows Jesus calling Andrew and Peter to follow him.*
*How can you be a good friend to Jesus and to others?*

# Jesus Asks Friends to Follow

One day Peter and his brother Andrew were fishing. Jesus passed by. He said to them, "Come, follow me. Learn how to help others. That will be your new work." Peter and Andrew left their work and followed Jesus. Jesus spoke to James and John. Jesus asked them to follow him. James and John left their work to follow Jesus too. *adapted from Mark 1:16–20*

## Jesus Asks Us to Follow

Long ago, Jesus asked the fishermen to follow him. Today he asks us. Peter, Andrew, James, and John were good friends to Jesus. We need good friends too. In the Church we can find friends who follow Jesus.

Draw a picture of yourself with your friends.

Name _____ Date _____

*Art Print 12 shows Jesus' friends receiving the Holy Spirit. How do you feel knowing that the Holy Spirit is with you?*

# The Holy Spirit Comes

One day, Jesus' friends were praying. Whoosh! A big wind came from the sky. It filled the house. They saw flames of fire, but they were not afraid. The Holy Spirit had come. Now they could tell the world about Jesus. We call this special day **Pentecost.**

*adapted from Acts of the Apostles 2:1–4*

## The Holy Spirit Brings Courage

Before this day Jesus' friends were afraid of people who did not like them. But then the Holy Spirit came. He gave them courage. They were not afraid to talk about Jesus anymore.

Color the symbols of the Holy Spirit.

### Reading God's Word

The Holy Spirit gives us love, kindness, and peace.

*adapted from Galatians 5:22*

Name _____ Date _____

*Art Print 13 shows a group of people riding on the subway.*
*How can you show the people around you that you care about them?*

## Our Neighbors

Who are our neighbors? They are the people
around us. God wants us to love them. We
show them love by sharing with them. This is
what Jesus did.

Complete the sentence below. Then draw a picture
of how you feel when you share with others.

I can share by _____

_____

_____ .

Name _____    Date _____

*Art Print 14 shows the angel Gabriel visiting Mary.*
*How can you say yes to God like Mary did?*

# An Angel Visits Mary

Mary lived long ago. One day an angel came to her. The angel's name was Gabriel. God sent Gabriel to Mary.

Gabriel said, "Do not be afraid. You will have a son. You will name him Jesus."

Mary said, "I will do what God wants." Mary said yes to God.

*adapted from Luke 1:26–38*

Color the picture of Mary and the angel Gabriel.

Name _____     Date _____

*Art Print 15 shows baby Jesus with Mary, Joseph, shepherds, angels, and animals. How can you spread the joy of Christmas all year long?*

# Celebrating Christmas

Christmas begins on Christmas Eve, December 24, and ends on the Sunday after the Feast of the Epiphany.

Three Wise Men believed that someday a star would tell the birth of the Son of God. They waited to see the star in the sky. When it finally came, they packed their camels with gifts and traveled for almost a year to reach Jesus. The Wise Men's long trip to see Jesus showed how important his birth was.

## The Gift of Jesus

The most important part of Christmas is the gift of Jesus. Jesus taught us to love one another and to love God most of all.

Write a prayer thanking God for giving us Jesus. Ask him to bless you and your family.

_____

_____

_____

_____

_____

_____

Name _____   Date _____

*Art Print 16 shows Jesus surrounded by children.*
*How can you live the way God wants you to live?*

# Jesus Loves Children

People brought children to see Jesus. But Jesus' friends said,
"Do not bother him with children."

Jesus heard this. He was upset. He said, "Bring the children
to me. They are very special people."

Jesus hugged the children. Then he blessed them.

*adapted from Mark 10:13–16*

All children are special to Jesus.
Look at the picture. How is Jesus
showing love? Write your answer
below. Then color the picture.

_____

_____

_____

_____

_____

_____

_____

Name _____ Date _____

*Art Print 17 shows Saint Peter, one of Jesus' best friends, who called others to follow Jesus. How do we become followers of Jesus?*

# Followers of Jesus

One day Peter was talking about Jesus.

Many people heard Peter's words.
They asked, "How can we follow Jesus?"

"Love God. Join his family," said Peter.

And many did as Peter said. They followed Jesus.
They joined God's family.

*adapted from Acts of the Apostles 2:37–41*

## We Are Invited

We are all invited to be followers of Jesus too. God loves everyone and wants us to be part of his family. We join God's family when we are baptized.

Color the pictures of Jesus and his disciples and the baby being baptized. Remember that you are a member of God's family.

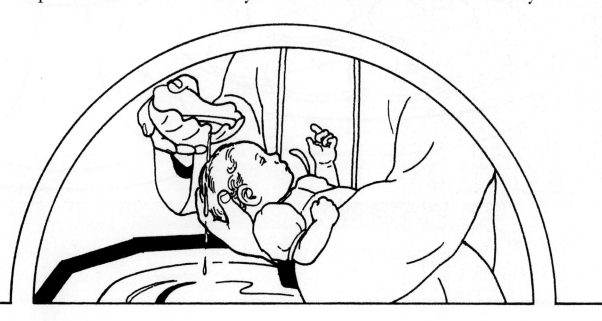

Name _____  Date _____

*Art Print 18 shows many people walking to church for Mass.*
*What is your favorite part of the Mass?*

# Mass, Our Special Meal

Every Sunday we go to Mass. What do we do at Mass?

► We remember Jesus.
► We have a special meal.
► We show our love for one another.

Before we leave Mass, the priest says important words.
He tells us to glorify God.

Color the special meal we have at Mass.

### Reading God's Word

Whatever you do, do it to praise God.

*adapted from 1 Corinthians 10:31*

Name _____    Date _____

*Art Print 19 shows three women singing and dancing.*
*How and when do you pray?*

# Praying to God

What do we tell God?
We tell him we are happy.
We tell him we are sad.
We can tell God anything!

How do we pray?
We use words.
We sing songs.
We use **gestures.**
We dance.
We listen to God.

Where can we pray?
We can pray at home.
We can pray at school.
We can pray in the car.
We can pray at church.
We can pray anywhere!

Draw a picture of yourself praying.

## Link to Liturgy

We can pray anytime and anywhere. We can pray about anything. We pray together at Mass.

Name _____   Date _____

*Art Print 20 shows Jesus on the cross.*
*How will you prepare your heart during Lent?*

# Celebrating Lent and Holy Week

Jesus spent his life praying and growing closer to God, his Father. As Christians we pray and learn about God. We want to be close to him. Jesus teaches us how to be closer to God.

- ▸ Jesus took care of those who were poor and sick.
- ▸ Jesus prayed.
- ▸ Jesus shared God's message with others.

The Lenten season reminds us to live as Jesus did. Each time we make a choice to be like Jesus, we grow closer to God.

Write a prayer asking God to help you always do your best. Tell him you will be more like Jesus during Lent.

_____

_____

_____

_____

_____

_____

Name _____ Date _____

*Art Print 21 shows a woman serving food to people in need.*
*What helps you make good decisions?*

# Good Decisions

How can we make good decisions? We can ask three questions.

Will my decision hurt anyone?

What does God want me to do?

Is this a good thing to do?

Write about a big decision you had to make. What happened?

_____

_____

_____

_____

## Reading God's Word

People asked Jesus, "What is the most important commandment?"
He said, "First, love God. Love him with all your heart, soul,
and mind. The second is like it: Love your neighbor as yourself."

*adapted from Matthew 22:36–39*

Name _____   Date _____

*Art Print 22 shows Jesus as the Good Shepherd. What can you do when you have turned away from God and are lost?*

# The Good Shepherd

Jesus told a story. He said,

Imagine you are a shepherd.
You have 100 sheep.
One gets lost.
You leave all your sheep.

You go to look for the lost one.
You look everywhere.
Then you finally find it.
You are so happy!

You carry the sheep home carefully.
You tell everyone that you found
    your lost sheep.

A person who does something wrong
    is like that lost sheep.
All of heaven is happy when that lost
    sheep is found.

*adapted from Luke 15:3–7*

Draw the correct path through the maze to help the lost sheep get home.

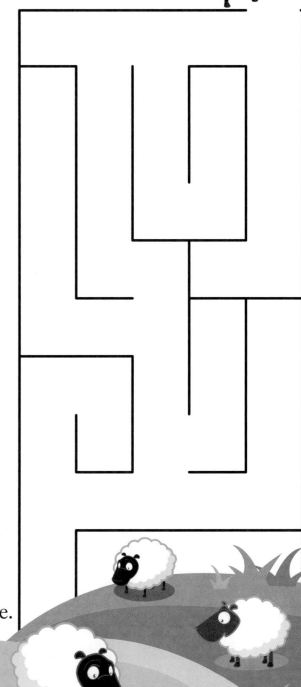

Name _____  Date _____

*Art Print 23 shows a family spending time together at a park. How do you like to spend time with your family?*

# God and Family

Your parents have loved you since before you were born. They want you to be healthy. They want you to be happy. They want the very best for you.

When you listen to your parents, God is happy. When you do what your parents ask you to do, God is happy. When you love your parents, God is happy.

Draw a picture that shows one way you can love your parents.

### Did You Know?

"Obey your parents" is a commandment. Jesus followed this commandment.

Name _____ Date _____

*Art Print 24 shows the Garden of Eden from the Bible.*
*Why is it important to take care of God's world?*

# The First Garden

God took the first man to a beautiful garden. He asked the man
to take care of it. Then God created different animals and birds.
God said to the man, "Give them names." So the man gave
names to the animals. And he gave names to the birds.

*adapted from Genesis 2:15,19–20*

Find Adam and Eve in the picture below and circle them.
Then write about your favorite thing in God's creation.

_____

_____

**Reading God's Word**

The land gives us food and flowers. Our God blesses us.

*adapted from Psalm 67:7*

Name _____ Date _____

*Art Print 25 shows the risen Jesus Christ and the women who went to the tomb Easter morning. How do you celebrate Easter?*

# Celebrating Easter

After Jesus died on the cross, he was laid in a tomb. Two women went to the tomb to honor him. They saw that Jesus' body was gone. But Jesus appeared to them and told them not to be afraid. The women were so happy.

On Easter we celebrate Jesus' rising from the dead. We sing and pray Alleluia!

Connect the dots to see where we can meet Jesus.

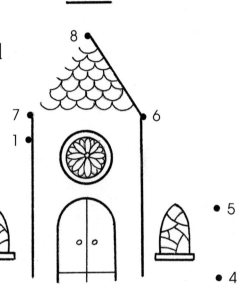

©LOYOLAPRESS.

# Glossary

## A

**absolution** the forgiveness of God. In the Sacrament of Penance and Reconciliation, we say that we are sorry for our sins. Then the priest offers us God's absolution. [absolución]

**Advent** the four weeks before Christmas. It is a time of joyful preparation for the celebration of Jesus' birth. [Adviento]

**All Saints Day** November 1, the day on which the Church honors all who have died and now live with God as saints in Heaven. These saints include all those who have been declared saints by the Church and many others known only to God. [Día de Todos los Santos]

**All Souls Day** November 2, the day on which the Church remembers all who have died as friends of God. We pray that they may rest in peace. [Día de los Fieles Difuntos]

**Alleluia** a prayer of praise to God. It is usually sung before the Gospel Reading at Mass. [Aleluya]

**altar** the table in the church on which the priest celebrates Mass. On this table the bread and wine are offered to God and become the Body and Blood of Jesus Christ. [altar]

**ambo** a platform from which a person reads the Word of God during Mass [ambón]

**Amen** the last word in any prayer that we pray. *Amen* means "This is true." We pray "Amen" to show that we really mean the words we have just said. [Amén]

**angel**  a messenger from God  [ángel]

**Ash Wednesday**  the first day of Lent. We receive ashes on our foreheads on this day to remind us to show sorrow for the choices we make that hurt our friendships with God and with others.  [Miércoles de Ceniza]

## B

**Baptism**  the first of the three sacraments by which we become members of the Church. Baptism frees us from Original Sin and gives us new life in Jesus Christ through the Holy Spirit.  [Bautismo]

**Beatitudes**  the eight ways we can behave in order to lead a Christian life. Jesus explains that if we live according to the Beatitudes, we are living as his followers.  [Bienaventuranzas]

**Bible**  the written story of God's promise to care for us, especially through his Son, Jesus  [Biblia]

**bishop**  a leader in the Church. Bishops teach us what God is asking of us as followers of Jesus today.  [obispo]

**Blessed Sacrament**  the Eucharist that has been consecrated by the priest at Mass. It is kept in the tabernacle to adore and to be taken to those who are sick.  [Santísimo Sacramento]

**Body and Blood of Christ**  the Bread and Wine that has been consecrated by the priest at Mass  [Cuerpo y Sangre de Cristo]

**Bread of Life** a title for Jesus that tells us he is the Bread, or food, for the faithful [pan de vida]

# C

**catholic** a word that means "all over the world." The Church is catholic because Jesus gave the Church to the whole world. [católico]

**celebrant** a bishop or priest who leads the people in praying the Mass [celebrante]

**celebrate** to praise and worship God in a special way [celebrar]

**chasuble** the visible liturgical vestment worn by the bishop or priest at Mass. The newly ordained priest receives a chasuble as part of the ordination ritual. [casulla]

**Christ** a title, like *Messiah*, that means "anointed with oil." It is the name given to Jesus after the Resurrection. [Cristo]

**Christian** the name given to people who want to live as Jesus taught us to live [cristiano]

**Christmas** the day on which we celebrate the birth of Jesus (December 25) [Navidad]

**Church** the name given to the followers of Christ all over the world. Spelled with a small *c*, *church* is the name of the building in which we gather to pray to God. [Iglesia]

**commandment** a rule that tells us how to live as God wants us to live [mandamiento]

**confession** the act of telling our sins to a priest in the Sacrament of Penance and Reconciliation [confesión]

**Confirmation** the sacrament that completes the grace we receive in Baptism [Confirmación]

**conscience** the inner voice that helps each of us know what God wants us to do [conciencia]

**consecration** the making of a thing or person to be special to God through prayer. At Mass the words of the priest are a consecration of the bread and wine. This makes them the Body and Blood of Jesus Christ. [consagración]

**contrition** the sadness we feel when we know that we have sinned [contrición]

**creation** everything that God has made. God said that all of creation is good. [creación]

**Creator** God, who made everything that is [Creador]

**crosier** the staff carried by a bishop. This staff shows that the bishop cares for us in the same way that a shepherd cares for his sheep. [báculo]

# D

**deacon** a man who accepts God's call to serve the Church. Deacons help the bishop and priests in the work of the Church. [diácono]

**disciple** a person who is a follower of Jesus and tries to live as he did [discípulo]

# E

**Easter** the celebration of the bodily raising of Jesus Christ from the dead. Easter is the most important Christian feast. [Pascua]

**Emmanuel** a name that means "God with us." It is a name given to Jesus. [Emanuel]

**eternal life** living happily with God in Heaven after we die [vida eterna]

**Eucharist** the sacrament in which we give thanks to God for giving us Jesus Christ [Eucaristía]

**Evangelists** the four men credited with writing the Gospels of Matthew, Mark, Luke, and John [evangelista]

**examination of conscience** thinking about what we have said or done that may have hurt our friendship with God or with others [examen de conciencia]

# F

**faith** a gift of God. Faith helps us to believe in God and live as he wants us to live. [fe]

**forgiveness** the act of being kind to people who have hurt us but then have said that they are sorry. God always forgives us when we say that we are sorry. We forgive others the way God forgives us. [perdón]

**Fruits of the Holy Spirit** the ways in which we act because God is alive in us [frutos del Espíritu Santo]

## G

**genuflect** to show respect in church by touching a knee to the ground, especially in front of the tabernacle [genuflexión, hacer la]

**gestures** the movements we make, such as the Sign of the Cross or bowing, to show our reverence during prayer [gestos]

**God** the Father, Son, and Holy Spirit. God created us, saves us, and lives in us. [Dios]

**godparent** a witness to Baptism. A godparent helps the baptized person to live as a follower of Jesus. [padrino/madrina de Bautismo]

**grace** the gift of God given to us without our earning it. Sanctifying grace fills us with God's life and makes us his friends. [gracia]

**Great Commandment** Jesus' important teaching that we are to love both God and other people [Mandamiento Mayor, el]

**guardian angel** the angel who has been appointed to help a person grow close to God [ángel de la guarda]

## H

**Heaven** the life with God that is full of happiness and never ends [cielo]

**holy** showing the kind of life we live when we cooperate with the grace of God  [santa]

**Holy Communion** The reception of the Body and Blood of Jesus Christ during Holy Mass [Sagrada Comunión]

**Holy Days of Obligation** those days other than Sundays on which we celebrate the great things God has done for us through Jesus Christ [días de precepto]

**Holy Family** the family made up of Jesus; his mother, Mary; and his foster father, Joseph  [Sagrada Familia]

**Holy Spirit** the third Person of the Trinity, who comes to us in Baptism and fills us with God's life [Espíritu Santo]

**holy water** water that has been blessed. It is used to remind us of our Baptism.  [agua bendita]

**Holy Week** the week that celebrates the events of Jesus' giving us the Eucharist, his suffering, Death, and Resurrection  [Semana Santa]

**Homily** an explanation of God's Word. The Homily explains the Word of God that we hear in the Bible readings at church.  [homilía]

**honor** giving to God or a person the respect that they are owed  [honrar]

**hope** the trust that God will always be with us. We also trust that he will make us happy now and help us to live in a way that keeps us with him forever.  [esperanza]

**J**

**Jesus** the Son of God, who was born of the Virgin Mary, died, was raised from the dead, ascended into Heaven, and saves us so that we can live with God forever [Jesús]

**Joseph** the foster father of Jesus, who was engaged to Mary when the angel announced that Mary would have a child through the power of the Holy Spirit [José]

**K**

**Kingdom of God** God's rule over us. We experience the Kingdom of God in part now. We will experience it fully in Heaven. [reino de Dios]

**L**

**Last Supper** the last meal Jesus ate with his disciples on the night before he died. Every Mass is a remembrance of that last meal. [Última Cena]

*Lectionary for Mass* the book from which the stories from the Bible are read at Mass [Leccionario]

**Lent** six weeks during which we prepare to celebrate, with special prayers and actions, the rising of Jesus from the dead at Easter. Jesus rose from the dead to save us. [Cuaresma]

**Light of the World** a name that helps us see that Jesus is the light that leads us to the Father [luz del mundo]

**liturgical year** the calendar that tells us when to celebrate the feasts of Jesus' birth, life, Death, Resurrection, and Ascension [año litúrgico]

**liturgy** the public prayer of the Church that celebrates the wonderful things God has done for us in Jesus Christ [liturgia]

**Liturgy of the Eucharist** a main part of the Mass in which the bread and wine are consecrated and become the Body and Blood of Jesus Christ. We receive the Body and Blood of Jesus Christ in Holy Communion. [Liturgia de la Eucaristía]

**Liturgy of the Word** a main part of the Mass in which we listen to God's Word from the Bible. [Liturgia de la Palabra]

## M

**Magnificat** Mary's song of praise to God. She praises him for the great things he has done for her and for his plans for us through Jesus. [Magníficat]

**Mary** the mother of Jesus. She is "full of grace" because God chose her to be Jesus' mother. [María]

**Mass** our most important means of praying to God. At Mass we listen to God's Word, the Bible. The bread and wine are consecrated and become the Body and Blood of Jesus Christ. [misa]

**Messiah** a title, like *Christ,* that means "anointed with oil." *Messiah* also means "Savior." [Mesías]

**ministry** the service, or work, done for others. Ministry is done by bishops, priests, and deacons in the celebration of the sacraments. All those baptized are called to different kinds of ministry in the liturgy and in serving the needs of others. [ministerio]

**miracle** the healing of a person, or an occasion when nature is controlled because of God's action [milagro]

**moral choice** a choice to do what is right. We make moral choices because they help us grow closer to God. [opción moral]

**mortal sin** a serious choice to turn away from God [pecado mortal]

**N**

**Nativity scene** a picture or crèche that shows Jesus, Mary, and Joseph in the stable after the birth of Jesus as described in the Gospels of Matthew and Luke [escena de la Natividad del Señor]

**neighbor** for a Christian, every other person, as each person is made in God's image [prójimo]

**New Testament** the story of Jesus and the early Church [Nuevo Testamento]

**O**

**obey** to follow the teachings given by God or by someone who has the right to direct us [obedecer]

**Old Testament** the story of God's plan for Salvation before the birth of Jesus [Antiguo Testamento]

**Ordinary Time** the longest liturgical season of the Church. It is divided into two periods—one after the Christmas season and one after Pentecost. [Tiempo Ordinario]

**Original Sin** the result of the sin of Adam and Eve. They disobeyed God and chose to follow their own will rather than God's will. [pecado original]

## P

**parable** one of the simple stories that Jesus told to show us what God wants for the world [parábola]

**parish** a community of believers in Jesus Christ who meet regularly to worship God together [parroquia]

**peacemaker** a person who teaches us to be respectful in our words and actions toward one another [paz, los que trabajan por la]

**penance** what we do to show we are turning away from sin so that we can live as God wants us to live (*See* Sacrament of Penance and Reconciliation.) [penitencia]

**Pentecost** the 50th day after Jesus was raised from the dead. On this day the Holy Spirit was sent from Heaven, and the Church was born. [Pentecostés]

**petition** a request we make to God, asking for what we need since we know that he created us and wants to give us what we need [petición]

**pope** the bishop of Rome, successor of Saint Peter, and leader of the Roman Catholic Church [Papa]

**praise** our telling of the happiness we feel simply because God is so good [alabanza]

**prayer** our talking to God and listening to him in our hearts [oración]

**priest** a man who accepts God's special call to serve the Church. Priests guide the Church and lead it in the celebration of the sacraments. [sacerdote]

## R

**reconciliation** making friends again after a friendship has been broken by some action or lack of action. In the Sacrament of Penance and Reconciliation, we are reconciled with God, the Church, and others. [Reconciliación]

**Resurrection** the bodily raising of Jesus Christ from the dead on the third day after he died on the cross [Resurrección]

**rite** the special form followed in celebrating each sacrament [rito]

## S

**sacrament** the way in which God enters our life. Through simple objects such as water, oil, and bread, Jesus continues to bless us. [sacramento]

**Sacrament of Penance and Reconciliation** the sacrament in which we celebrate God's forgiveness of our sins when we say to the priest that we are sorry for them [sacramento de la Penitencia y de la Reconciliación]

**Sacraments of Initiation** the sacraments that make us members of God's Church. They are Baptism, Confirmation, and the Eucharist. [sacramentos de iniciación]

**Sacrifice of the Mass** remembering the sacrifice of Jesus on the cross. We remember Jesus' sacrifice every time we celebrate Mass. [Sacrificio de la misa]

**saint** a holy person who has died as a true friend of God and now lives with God forever [santo]

**Savior** Jesus, the Son of God, who became man to make us friends with God again. *Jesus* means "God saves." [Salvador]

**seal of confession** refers to the fact that the priest must keep absolutely secret the sins that are confessed to him in the Sacrament of Penance and Reconciliation [sigilo sacramental]

**Sign of Peace** the part of the Mass in which we offer a gesture of peace to one another as we prepare to receive Holy Communion [rito de la paz]

**sin** a choice we make that hurts our friendships with God and with other people [pecado]

**Son of God** the name given to Jesus that reveals his special relationship to God the Father [Hijo de Dios]

## T

**tabernacle** the container in which the Blessed Sacrament is kept so that Holy Communion can be taken to those who are sick [sagrario]

**Temple** the Temple in Jerusalem, the most important place where the Jewish people came to pray. They believed that this was the place where they could be closest to God. Jesus often came to pray in the Temple. [Templo, judío]

**temptation** a thought or feeling that can lead us to disobey God. Temptation can come either from outside us or inside us. [tentación]

**Ten Commandments** the ten rules that God gave to Moses. The Ten Commandments sum up God's law and show us how to live as his children. [Diez Mandamientos]

**transubstantiation** when the bread and wine become the Body and Blood of Jesus Christ [transubstanciación]

**trespasses** acts that harm others [ofensas]

**Trinity** the mystery of one God existing in three Persons: the Father, the Son, and the Holy Spirit [Trinidad]

## V

**venial sin** a choice we make that weakens our relationships with God or with other people [pecado venial]

# Index

## A

absolution, 239
Adam, 236
Advent, 27, 57–60, 152, 153–56, 222, 239
Advent wreath, 155
All Saints Day, 152, 177–78, 239
All Souls Day, 239
Alleluia, 119, 149, 239
altar, 199, 239
altar server, 198
ambo, 198, 239
Amen, 6, 239
Andrew, Saint, 223
angel, 34, 52, 240
    guardian angel, 65, 244
    Mary visited by, 32, 226
Annunciation, 32, 226
Anointing of the Sick, Sacrament
    of the, 196
apologizing, 220.
      *See also* forgiveness
apostle, 76
Ash Wednesday, 117, 118, 163, 240

## B

Baptism, Sacrament of, 100, 103–4,
    194, 240
    godparents and, 101
    welcome into God's family, 102
Beatitudes, 240
Bible, 17, 184–85, 240
    God's message in, 17, 18, 20
bishop, 240
Blessed Sacrament, 240
blessing, 100
Body and Blood of Christ, 107, 110,
    240, 245
bread and wine, 29, 107, 110, 245
Bread of Life, 241

## C

calendar, 27. *See also* liturgical calendar
caring
    Jesus cares for us, 129–34
    for others and God's world, 9–14, 139,
      142, 143, 145, 146
catholic, 241
Catholic Church. *See* Church, the
celebrant, 90, 241
celebrate, 241
celebration
    Christmas, 87–90
    Easter, 147–50
    of our faith, 194–97
chalice, 199
chasuble, 199, 241
children, Jesus loves, 228
children of God, 179
Christ, 52, 150, 241. *See also* Jesus
Christian, 77, 241
Christmas, 27, 87–90, 152, 157, 227, 241
Christmas tree, 89
Church, the, 64–65, 67–68, 77, 80, 241
    church, as building, 241
    holy water, 103
    statue of Mary in, 83
"Come, O Holy Spirit, Wa Wa Wa
    Emimimo" (song), 210
"Come All You People" (song), 211
commandment, 124–26, 128, 242.
      *See also* Ten Commandments
    Great Commandment, 202, 244
community, 203
confession, 242, 251
Confirmation, Sacrament of, 195, 242
conscience, 242, 243
consecration, 242
contrition, 242
creation, 205, 242
    caring for, 141–46
    gift from God, 4, 141
    perfection of, 13